J. B. McClure

Stories, Sketches and Speeches of General Grant

At Home and Abroad, in Peace and in War

J. B. McClure

Stories, Sketches and Speeches of General Grant
At Home and Abroad, in Peace and in War

ISBN/EAN: 9783744659802

Printed in Europe, USA, Canada, Australia, Japan

Cover: Foto ©ninafisch / pixelio.de

More available books at **www.hansebooks.com**

STORIES, SKETCHES

AND SPEECHES

OF

GENERAL GRANT

AT HOME AND ABROAD, IN PEACE AND IN WAR.

INCLUDING

HIS TRIP AROUND THE WORLD, AND ALL THE INTERESTING
INCIDENTS, ANECDOTES, AND IMPORTANT EVENTS
OF HIS LIFE.

EDITED BY

J. B. McCLURE,

Compiler of "Moody's Anecdotes;" "Moody's Child Stories;" "Edison and His Inventions;" "Entertaining Anecdotes;" "Mistakes of Ingersoll;" "Lincoln's Stories," Etc., Etc.

CHICAGO:
RHODES & McCLURE, PUBLISHERS.
1879.

Entered according to Act of Congress, in the year 1879,

BY RHODES & McCLURE,

In the office of the Librarian of Congress, at Washington, D. C.

Electrotyped and Printed by	Bound by
OTTAWAY & CO.,	KINGSBURY & WILSON,
147 & 149 Fifth Ave., Chicago.	202 Clark Street, Chicago.

Preface

We are specially indebted, in the preparation of this volume, to the writings of Messrs. Deming, Coppee, Headley, Badeau, Larke, and John Russell Young; also to the press and friends. It is perhaps quite true that General Grant has received more homage from the civilized world than any other man in the world's history. These Stories and Sketches, and we may add, Speeches, constitute, in fact, a very readable and exhaustive sketch-life of the world-renowned General. With a desire to disseminate and perpetuate what is good and noble in the truly great, the volume is submitted.

J. B. McCLURE.

CHICAGO, November 10, 1879.

A

Anecdote of Grant at West Point.. 41
A Remarkable Incident of Young Grant's Integrity—He Buys a
    Horse for His Father—All About the Bargain................ 22
An Inaugural Extract.. 140
A Confederate's Graphic Story of the Battle of Iuka............ 120
A Speech of Gen. Grant over 2,000 Miles Long—From San Francisco to Galena—What He Said................................. 204
Address of General Grant to the Workingmen..................... 154
Address to the Working People....................................... 180
Ascending Mt. Vesuvius... 156
At Burlington 206
At Fremont... 205
At Galesburg 207
At Home.. 207
At Omaha... 206
At Pompeii 164
At Sacramento.. 205

D

Down in the Mines at Virginia City................................. 201

E

Explosion of the Great Vicksburg Mine and Capture of that City, 122

F

Farewell to San Francisco... 205

CONTENTS.

G

General Grant's Birth and Early Surroundings—A Noble Line of Ancestry—His Father and Mother	28
General Grant at School—How He Mastered His Lessons—The Young Leader—His Early Character	21
General Grant's Early Love for Horses—His Experience in "Breaking In" a Colt—He Masters the "Ribbons" in His Ninth Year	18
General Grant's First Gun—Fired when a Two-Year Old Baby—He is Delighted with the "Pop," and Wants them to "Fick it Again"	17
General Grant's Capture of a "Willing Prisoner"—Her Name was "Miss Julia"—His Marriage—Social Life in Detroit	80
General Grant and President Lincoln in Washington	131
General Grant's Address	121
General Grant's own Description of the Battle of Fort Donelson	104
General Grant's Private Letter to his Father, Describing the Opening Battle at Belmont	102
General Grant's Private Letter to Sherman on the Lieutenant-Generalship	130
General Grant's Words to the "Grand Army"	109
General Grant as a Farmer—He Buys a Farm and Settles Down Near St. Louis	88
General Grant's First "Baptism in Blood"—The American Columns Torn to Pieces before Fort Teneria—Tunnelling Walls and Fighting on Roofs of Houses—Grant "Foremost in the Ranks"	53
General Grant's First Battle—Called from the Swamps of Louisiana to the Plains of Mexico—At Palo Alto and Resaca—Leaping Into the "Ravine of Palms"—His Grand Bayonet Charge	50
General Grant's First Half Year of War—It Opens on Fields of Sublimest Imagery, but they are Storied in Human Sacrifice and Midnight Superstitions—Grant Amid Pyramids, Smoking Mountains, and on the Heights of Chapultepec	61
General Grant's First Official Compliments as a Soldier—The First "Brevet"	56
General Grant's First Siege—He Personally Supervises Twelve Miles of Trench and Parallel, from which he Shatters the Enemy's Redoubts and Bastions	55
General Grant and Prince Bismarck—An Interesting Interview between Two Remarkably Great Men	173

General Grant's Celebrated Liverpool Speech...................... 152
Gen. Grant's Great Speech in Birmingham...................... 183
General Grant in Paris... 155
General Grant's Reception in Salford and Leicester.............. 147
Gen. Grant's Return... 192
General Grant's Speech in London, and Private Letter to a Friend
   in America, Describing His Travels........................ 148
General Grant's Class-mates at West Point—Who they Were, and
   What they have Done—An Interesting Biographical Series.. 45
General Grant in Oregon—Watching the Indians................. 83
General Lee's Generous Compliment to General Grant........... 138
General Lee's Surrender to General Grant—The Decisive Letters
   which Ended the Rebellion—Grant's own Account of his
   Meeting Lee.. 132
General Smith's Graphic Description of Grant's Galena Life—
   Laughable Reception by his Regiment...................... 93
Governor Yates' Story of How Grant Got into the Army....... 96
Grant's First Movements in the Great Rebellion, and his First
   Little Speech.. 99
Grant as a Citizen of Illinois—His Life in Galena—What he Knows
   About Leather... 91
Grant's Speech in Glasgow 177
Grape and Canister—Fired at Random—Many Interesting Little
   Things About Young Grant................................. 32
Greece and Rome 185

H

How General Grant Received the Name "Hiram Ulysses"—And
   How the Change was Made to "Ulysses Simpson"—And then
   to "Uncle Sam "... 24

I

In Constantinople.. 168
In Edinburgh 176
In Egypt... 162
In Jerusalem... 170
In Russia 186
In the Orient 188
In the Yosemite Valley—The " Loveliest Panorama Ever Seen "—
   Grant's Little Stories.................................... 194

L

Let us Have Peace" 178
Lieutenant-General Grant's Farewell Address to the Soldiers..... 137
Lieutenant Grant Witnessing General Scott's Triumphal Entry into the City of Mexico—What He Sees from the Grand Plaza. 76

O

Off for Europe—General Grant's Good-Bye to Old Friends........ 142
On a Foreign Shore—General Grant's Arrival in Liverpool—The Welcome Words—His Address in Manchester.................. 144
On to Mexico—Grant's First Experience in Capturing a Capital—A Great and Glittering City Approached by the High-ways of Death—Grant's Active Part in the Dreadful Struggle......... ·65

P

President Lincoln's Congratulations to General Grant, and Lincoln's Little Joke.. 129
President Grant—Closing Scenes in the White House—His Opinion of his own Administration......................... 141

Q

Queen Victoria and General Grant at Dinner—A Very Happy Affair.. 153

R

Remarkable Instance of Grant's Generalship at the Age of Twelve —How He Loaded Big Logs all Alone—His Father's Surprise 25

S

Speech at Newcastle.. 178
Speech in Brighton... 184
Speech in Sheffield—Grant's First Penknife 182

T

The First "Flank Movement"—An Opposing Army which Grant Thought Best to Pass Around, with Heavy Margins, to "the Left"—Scaling the Heights of Cerro Gordo.................. 58

CONTENTS.

The Race—Parallel Generals—On a Four-Year Race Grant Comes in Ahead 108
The Reported Story that Grant Borrowed Money in Galena to Equip Himself for the War 98
The Science of War—General Scott is Grant's Teacher—Theory vs. Practice 77
The Shiloh Victory, as Described by an Eye-witness 111
The Siege of Corinth—An eloquent Description by a Participant.. 117

V

Vicksburg's Surrender—An Interesting Interview Between General Grant and the Confederate General, Pemberton 127

W

What a Fellow Comrade says of Young Grant at West Point—A Splendid Record 42
Young Grant and the Ladies—Escorting Under Immense Difficulties 32

Y

Young Grant's First Victory—He Accepts a Ring-master's Challenge to Ride the "Circus Pony"—An Exciting Occasion to Everybody but Grant 19
Young Grant a Cadet at West Point—An Interesting Account of His Life at that Institution 36

CLASSIFICATION

Boyhood	17
At West Point	36
In Mexico	50
Gen. Grant's Marriage	80
In the Far West	83
The Farmer	88
In Illinois	91
In the Rebellion	96
As President	140
Around the World	144

ILLUSTRATIONS

Banks of the Nile	145
Birthplace of General Grant	29
Capitol at Washington	140
Cascades	85
Cathedral at Strasburg	174
Constantinople	169
"Dave"	27
Departed Glory	165
Egypt	163
Elephant Worship in the East	180
En Route	16
Examination at West Point	43
Frontispiece	4
General Grant After his Return	193
Going to the Store	91
Grant on Horseback	23
Interior Great Cathedral, City of Mexico	67
Jephthah's Vow	171
Mirror Lake, Yosemite	197
Naples and Mt. Vesuvius	157
Napoleon Witnessing the Burning of Moscow	187
President Grant Reviewing the Cadets at West Point—His Old Playground Thirty Years Before	37
Storm	123
Street in Cairo	167
Summit of Popocatapetl	59
The Domes, etc., Yosemite	199
The Old World	149
The Pyramid of Cholula	62
The State Capitol at Springfield, Ill.	94

ILLUSTRATIONS. 15

Tropical Climes.. 51
Tropical Gardens.. 75
Ulysses and his Colt... 18
Unforgotten 97
Venice 179
Victory.. 20
War in Ancient Times... 106
Wild Elephants.. 191

EN ROUTE.

STORIES AND SKETCHES

—OF—

GENERAL GRANT,

BOYHOOD.

General Grant's First Gun—Fired when a Two-Year Old Baby— He is Delighted with the "Pop" and Wants them to "Fick it again."

When General Grant was but two years old, his father one day "took him in his arms and carried him through the village for the purpose of giving young Ulysses some fresh air and also allowing him to enjoy the benefits of a little martial music in connection with a "public parade" being given by the villagers at the time.

A young gentleman of military bearing soon "sighted" the "coming General" and was seized by the strange infatuation of trying the effect of a pistol shot on young Ulysses' ears. After due consultation, the father consented, though as he said, "the child had never seen a gun or pistol in his life."

The young gentleman now presented his loaded pistol and the baby-fingers were accordingly pressed upon the trigger and he was told to "pull away," when the weapon was quickly discharged with a tremendous *bang !*

The little fellow exhibited no alarm whatever, neither winking nor dodging, but presently pushed the pistol away, and called out in his childish way : "*Fick it again, fick it again.*"

The wondering villagers, we are credibly informed, detected the future warrior in the marvelous composure which young Grant exhibited on this, his first experience "under fire."

General Grant's Early Love for Horses — His Experience in "Breaking In" a Colt — He Masters "The Ribbons" in His Ninth Year.

From General Grant's father we learn that young Ulysses first and "ruling passion," almost from the time he could "go alone," was for horses.

ULYSSES AND HIS COLT.

When only seven and a half years old, on a certain occasion, he took advantage of his father's absence from home for a day, to harness up a three-year old colt, which though accustomed to the saddle, had never before had a "collar on !" Young Ulysses not only succeeded in harnessing the vigorous little horse, but he hitched him up in first-class style to a sled which was on the premises, and spent the whole delightful day in hauling brush. This was a wonderful feat for so small a boy.

By the time he was eight, he could ride a horse at full speed bare-back and standing on one foot; at eight and a half years, he was a regular " driver " in all senses of that word, hauling wood for his father and making himself generally useful; and at ten years of age we find him in charge of a " spanking pair " of horses which, on a certain occasion, he drove forty miles down to Cincinnati, all alone, returning with a full load of cash-paying customers!

In the words of his father, " Whatever he undertook to ride he *rode*," and nothing could shake him off. He early began to break horses himself and developed a wonderful faculty for teaching them to "*pace* "—a knack which would have given him plenty of work from the neighbors, if he had not considered it rather degrading to do it for money and accordingly he refused to accommodate them.

Young Grant's First Victory—He Accepts a Ring-master's Challenge to Ride the "Circus Pony"—An Exciting Occasion to Everybody but Grant.

An anecdote is dropped by the paternal gossip, which deserves to be preserved as a graphic description of a scene through which many smart lads have passed, and as indicating in this particular instance some of that pluck, and tenacity of will, which distinguished the Wilderness campaign.

" Once, when he was a boy, a show came along, in which there was a mischievous pony, trained to go round the ring like lightning; and he was expected to throw any boy that attempted to ride him.

"'Will any boy come forward and ride this pony?' shouted the ring-master.

"Ulysses stepped forward, and mounted the pony.

"The performance began. Round and round and round the ring went the pony, faster and faster, making the greatest effort to dismount the rider; but Ulysses sat as steady as if he had grown to the pony's back.

"Presently out came a large monkey, and sprang up behind Ulysses. The people set up a great shout of laughter, and on the pony ran; but it all produced no effect on the rider.

"Then the ring-master made the monkey jump up on to Ulysses' shoulders, standing with his feet on his shoulders, and with his hands holding on to his hair.

"At this, there was another and a still louder shout; but not a muscle of Ulysses' face moved; there was not a tremor of his nerves.

"A few more rounds, and the ring-master gave it up; he had come across a boy that the pony and the monkey both could not dismount."

Young Grant dismounted amid the deafening plaudits of the multitude calm, cool and conscious of victory!

VICTORY!

BOYHOOD. 21

General Grant at School—How He Mastered His Lessons—The Young Leader—His Early Character.

Young Grant at school supplied his want of quickness by a dogged diligence which demanded, in every case, the "unconditional surrender" of his tasks. He always attacked a knotty question with "slow, but sure," approaches. When temporarily thwarted always "fought it out on that line," until he eventually won.

It is said on good authority, that he told his teacher one day—in view no doubt of some stupendous undertaking—that the word "can't" was not in his dictionary.

He frequently committed to memory whole pages which he did not understand, with the comfortable assurance that they would not be wasted upon his maturer intellect. In fact, the genuine manliness of his feelings, and the dignity of his deportment, when a boy at school, prognosticated the sterling characteristics which the man veils under a charitable spirit and an unpretending demeanor.

It is said that an astounded phrenologist, who, during these early days, on a certain occasion, while manipulating the young General's cranium, exclaimed with prophetic emphasis: "You need not be surprised, if at some day this boy fills the Presidential chair."

As a boy "out of school" young Grant seems to have been as modest, retiring, and reticent as he has been in his subsequent career; yet he always manifested a proper amount of confidence in his ability to do any thing which was to be expected of a boy of his size and years. Among boys he was regarded as a leader; yet, without forwardness, he rather sought the company of older persons.

His disposition was peaceable, yet would stand no imposition upon what he considered his rights; and when forced into a corner could fight as well as any one. The current story of his "flogging a captain" is, on his own authority, untrue; and it is said by those who know him well, that he never had a *personal* controversy in his life. Profanity was a vice which he was peculiarly free from, both in boyhood and in his subsequent military career.

A Remarkable Incident of Young Grant's Integrity—He Buys a Horse for His Father—All About the Bargain.

A popular story which was current among young Grant's companions, and which to a remarkable degree illustrates his honesty, was concerning a *horse trade* in which he was engaged.

It appears that when he was about twelve years of age, his father sent him to purchase a horse of a farmer, named Ralston, who resided some short distance in the country. The elder Grant wanted the horse, but still desired to get it as cheaply as possible. Before starting, the old gentleman impressed upon young Grant's mind that fact in these words :

" Ulysses, when you see Mr. Ralston, tell him ᴧ have sent you to buy his horse, and offer him fifty dollars for it. If he will not take that, offer him fifty-five dollars; and rather than you should come away without the horse, you had better give him sixty dollars."

Off started the boy, and in due course of time arrived at Ralston's farm-house. He had carefully studied over in his mind his father's instructions, and of course intended to do as his parent had told him. Mr. Ralston, however, threw him off his balance, by putting the following direct but natural question to him :

" How much did your father tell you to give for him ?"

Young Ulysses had always had it impressed upon his mind by his mother, that the truth must be spoken at all times, and therefore he replied :

"ULYSSES RODE THE HORSE HOME."

"Why, father told me to offer you fifty dollars at first; and that if that would not do, to give you fifty-five dollars; and rather than come away without the horse I was to pay sixty dollars."

Of course Ralston could not sell the horse for less than sixty dollars.

"I am sorry for that," 'returned Grant, "for, on looking at the horse, I have determined not to give more than fifty dollars for it, although father said I might give sixty. You may take fifty if you like, or you may keep the horse."

Ulysses rode the horse home!

How General Grant Received the Name "Hiram Ulysses"— And How the Change was Made to "Ulysses Simpson"—And then to "Uncle Sam."

According to the testimony of the father, the maternal grandmother of General Grant was greatly fascinated with the exploits of the wily Ithican chief who introduced the famous wooden horse into Troy and was anxious that the first born of Jesse's house should be named Ulysses.

The maternal grandfather, it is said was equally captivated with Tyrian history and was determined that the child should be christened Hiram.

This family jar was finally compromised by bestowing upon the coming General the names of both of the old people's heroes; and he was accordingly called Hiram Ulysses.

This name he bore until he was seventeen years of age, at which time he was recommended to the Secretary of War by the Hon. Thomas L. Hamer, a member of Congress from Ohio, for a cadetship in West Point, by the name of Ulysses Simpson Grant.

This serious mistake on the part of the Congressman, it

is said, was occasioned by the fact that Simpson was the maiden name of General Grant's mother and also the Christian name of one of the General's brothers. But from whatever cause the mistake may have occurred, to Ulysses S. Grant the commission was issued, appointing him to the Military Academy, and by this name he was entered upon its roster.

Young Grant afterwards applied to the authorities at West Point and the Secretary of War to have the blunder corrected, but his companions and the eternal fitness of things were against him. His request was unnoticed. His comrades at once adopted the initials U. S. in his behalf and christened him " *Uncle Sam*," a nickname that he never lost; and when he graduated in 1843, twenty-first, in a class of thirty-nine, his commission of brevet second lieutenant and his diploma, both styled him Ulysses S. Grant, by which name he has since been known.

Remarkable Instance of Grant's Generalship at the Age of Twelve —How He Loaded Big Logs all Alone— His Father's Surprise,

An anecdote is related by General Grant's father concerning young Ulysses which aptly illustrates the " grit" of the " coming General," as well as the faculty of adaptation of circumstances.

Mr. Grant, who had a contract for building the Brown County jail, had need of a number of logs some fourteen feet in length, and Ulysses, then in his twelfth year, volunteered to drive the team until the logs were hauled, if his father would purchase a certain horse which he thought an excellent match for another which he then owned.

His father consented and young Ulysses began work.

One cloudy April morning when rain was threatened,

Ulysses went as usual for his load. After a long trip, he came back with his logs, and as Jesse—his father—and the hired man were unloading them, he remarked :

"Father, it's hardly worth while for me to go again to-day; none of the hewers are in the woods. There is only one load left; if I get that now there will be none for me to haul in the morning."

"Where are the hewers?"

"At home, I suppose. They haven't been in the woods this morning."

"Who loaded these logs?"

"Dave and me." (Dave was the name of the horse.)

"What do you mean by telling me such a story?" asked the clear-headed father.

"It is the truth. I loaded the logs with no help but Dave's."

It was the truth. For this hauling, the body of the wagon had been removed and the logs were carried upon the axles. It was a hard job for several men to load. They would take the wheels off on one side, let the axles down to the ground, lift on the squared logs with hand spikes, then pry the axles up with levers, and put the wheels on again. That a mere boy could do this alone was incredible, and Jesse inquired :

"How in the world did you load the wagon?"

"Well, Father, you know that sugar tree we saw yesterday which is half fallen, and lies slanting, with the top caught in another tree, I hitched Dave to the logs, and drew them up on that; then backed the wagon up to it and hitched Dave to them again, and one at a time, snaked them forward upon the axles."

The ingenious lad had used the trunk of the fallen tree, as an inclined plane, and after hauling the logs upon it, so that they nearly balanced, had drawn them endwise upon

"DAVE."

his wagon underneath with little difficulty. The feat made him quite celebrated in the neighborhood.

It indicates a tendency to supplement physical weakness by head work. It is one of the most significant incidents related of his boyhood. It strongly foreshadows a disposition not to be thwarted by trifles; a precocious superiority to mere obstacles, which, when fully developed, might be expected to overcome those difficulties which are pronounced insurmountable.

General Grant's Birth and Early Surroundings—A Noble Line of Ancestry—His Father and Mother.

Ulysses S. Grant was born April 27, 1822, in an humble frame cottage, at Point Pleasant, Clermont County, Ohio, near the mouth of the Miami on the northern bank of the Ohio River, about twenty-five miles above Cincinnati.

Here he grew up to years of discretion amid the changeful skies, variable climate and productions, of the northern half of the temperate zone. His first tottering steps were unquestionably bounded by his father's tannery, which is presumed to have been within convenient distance of the paternal abode. He peers with the big eyes of wonder into the curious mysteries of the tan vats; he gazes, doubtless with mute astonishment at the towering steamboat, puffing spasmodically as its huge mass plows the Ohio.

Like innumerable other boys, with more or less fancy his uninitiated eye begins, gradually, to admire the shifting scenery of the heavens as sinking day brings out the more splendid pageant of the night, until the stars in turn, one by one, fade away before the purpling dawn. He exults in the voice of spring, the song of birds, the green luxuriance of summer, the golden abundance of the harvest, the masquerading attire of the autumnal forests. He pines, too, perhaps at the falling leaf, the wailing winds, the naked tree-tops, the morning frosts, the white fall of snow descending on the fading landscape, and the dancing and murmuring waters which he loved, wrapped in the chilling embrace of the ice.

General Grant is connected with a noble line of ancestry. He is descended from an ancient and worthy Connecticut

BIRTHPLACE OF GEN. GRANT.

family, the immigrant ancestor of which was Matthew Grant, who came over from England in 1630, in the ship "Mary and John," and with his fellow-passengers founded the town of Dorchester (now South Boston), Mass.

In 1636 he was one of the company who settled the town of Windsor, Connecticut, and was an active and prominent citizen, being a notable land surveyor, a faithful and remarkably conscientious town clerk and an influential member of the Church.

His great-grandson, Noah Grant, located at Tolland, Connecticut, and *his* son Noah removed to Coventry, about 1750, and was a Captain in the Crown Point Expedition of 1755, in which he and his brother Solomon were killed. His son Noah, General Grant's grandfather, was a lieutenant of militia at the battle of Lexington, in 1776, and served in the Continental Army during the entire Revolutionary War.

He removed from Coventry to Westmoreland County, Pennsylvania, about 1787, and there married, as his second wife, Rachel Kelley, in 1791. His son by this second marriage, Jesse Root Grant, the father of the hero, was born in Westmoreland County, in 1794, from whence, when he was five years of age, the family removed to what is now Columbiana County, Ohio ; and again, when he was ten years old, to Deerfield, Portage County, in the Western Reserve.

His father dying the next year, 1805, the family became somewhat scattered ; and during the War of 1812, Jesse, with his mother and the younger children, removed to Maysville, Kentucky ; the northern part of Ohio being unsafe for women and children, on account of the dangers from the British and their Indian allies. In 1815, being then of age, he established himself at Ravenna, Ohio, in the tanning business, to which he had served a full apprenticeship. Driven from thence in 1820 by the prevalence of the fever and ague, he removed to Point Pleasant, Clermont County, Ohio, on the Ohio River, twenty-five miles above Cincinnati; and there, in June of the same year, he married Hannah, daughter of John Simpson, who some three years previous had removed thither from Montgomery County, Pennsylvania.

Of good family, domestic in her habits, cheerful in disposition, and possessing great firmness and steadiness of character, as well as being a consistent member of the Methodist Church, she was well fitted to be the mother of children, and to influence their lives in the right and noblest direction.

General Grant, like many other great men, owes more than the world can ever tell, to the influence of a noble mother.

The portrait of General Grant's mother has been etched by her husband's hand in the following words: "At the time of our marriage, Mrs. Grant was an unpretending country girl—handsome, but not vain. She had previously joined the Methodist Church; and I can truthfully say that it has never had a more devoted and consistent member. Her steadiness, firmness, and strength of character, have been the stay of the family through life. She was always careful and most watchful over her children; but never austere, and not opposed to their free participation in innocent amusement."

Young Grant and the Ladies — Escorting Under Immense Difficulties.

General Grant, when but a boy, exhibited a remarkable self-possession of mind. It is related that on one occasion when driving a couple of lady passengers in a two-horse wagon across a creek in which he found the water very much deeper than he had expected—the creek was much swollen—and finding suddenly that the horses were swimming and the water up to a level with the wagon box, the ladies became greatly alarmed and began to scream at the top of their voices, but young Ulysses, though in a very dangerous situation for himself and his lady passengers, was not in the least thrown off his balance; he simply looked over his shoulder as he sat on the front seat holding the reins, and quietly said : *" Don't speak—I will take you through safe,"* and he did.

In these incidents of his boyish days we see a gleam of the same spirit that led him, in after years, when the whole country were looking on, to say: " I propose to fight it out on this line, if it takes all Summer."

Grape and Canister—Fired at Random—Many Interesting Little Things About Young Grant.

The first book read by young Ulysses—near the age of seven—was the " Life of General George Washington !"

It may be said of Grant's genealogy, as has been said of that of another distinguished American : " It discloses no crime and no disgrace; but also no eminence."

Mr. Everett's well-turned allusion to the family tree of General Washington may equally be applied to General

Grant: "The glory he reflected upon his ancestors was greater than he could inherit."

General Grant is of Scotch descent, and in those qualities which distinguish him shows that the Scotch blood still flows strongly through his veins.

As far as research has been able to recover the characteristics of the Grant family, they appear to have been a hard-working, earnest, upright, conscientious and law-abiding race.

Noah Grant, the grandfather of Ulysses, served with distinction during the entire Revolutionary War and after its conclusion, removed to Westmoreland County, Penn., where, on January 23, 1794, General Grant's father, Jesse Root Grant, was born.

The name of General Grant's mother before marriage was Hanna Simpson, daughter of John Simpson, of Montgomery County, Penn. In her nineteenth year she emigrated with her father to Clermont County, Ohio. She was married to Jesse Root Grant, June 24, 1821.

Grant's cadet warrant was made out for "ULYSSES SIDNEY," but he changed this to ULYSSES SIMPSON, in honor of his mother.

When Gov. Yates proposed sending the name of Grant to Washington for the appointment of Brigadier-General —early in the war—Grant refused his consent, curtly replying: "He did not want promotion; he wanted to earn it."

It is said of young Grant that he never had any personal quarrels with any one. He was quiet and inoffensive, but was not to be out-witted at a bargain.

Grant's education, previous to entering West Point, was quite limited. It was only in the mid-winter months that his father could spare him for school. This was enough, however, to implant a desire for a more thorough education, which young Ulysses obtained at the West Point Military Academy.

Unlike Napoleon, we hear nothing of young Grant "attacking snow forts," but he developed very early the faculty of "overcoming difficulties which would have checked other boys."

If Napoleon could rebuke the genealogist who was creating for him a pedigree, with the words: "Friend, my patent dates from Monte Notte," Grant may claim his American nobility from Fort Donelson.

When the fall of Fort Sumter startled the nation, Grant, who was in Galena, said: "Uncle Sam educated me for the army, and although I have served faithfully through one war, I feel that I am still a little in debt for my education, and I am ready to discharge it and *put down this rebellion.*"

In his "Life of General U. S. Grant" Henry C. Deming aptly remarks: "I am rejoiced to find that Grant was undoubtedly one of that number of illustrious men whose character received its first and most essential impress from maternal influence. In the early and susceptible years of childhood, from a mother's lips, he imbibes those simple yet fundamental maxims and principles which are the enduring foundation of all wise conduct in life, all good institutions in human society. The love of truth, the sentiment of honor, fidelity, obedience, constancy, are practical lessons alike for the lisping child, the aspiring youth, the busy man—at home, in the school, on the farm, at the head of the army, in the councils of the nation. As in the realm of Nature the components of the material world are reduced by analysis to a few simple elements, upholding, illuminating, fructifying the whole universe by the simple and omnipresent influences of gravity, heat, and light, so all the institutions of society, and all the relations of kindred, friend, and country, are inspired and regulated by a few homely truths of universal application.

Young Grant's mental development is an argument favoring mathematics as a mental discipline. He is said to have excelled only in this branch of study.

There are some men in this world possessing immense mental power, who yet, from inertness, pass through life with poor success. Lighter natures outstrip them in the race for wealth or position, and the strength they really possess is never known, because it has never been called out. It never *is* called out by ordinary events. They were made for great emergencies, and if these do not arise, they seem almost made in vain; at least these extraordinary powers to be given them in vain. Grant is one of these. He is like a great wheel on which mere rills of water may drop forever without moving it, or if they succeed in disturbing its equilibrium, only make it accomplish a partial revolution. It needs an immense body of water to make it roll, and then it revolves with a power and majesty that awes the beholder. No slight obstruction can arrest its sweep. Acquiring momentum with each revolution, it crushes to atoms everything thrust before it to check its motion.

AT WEST POINT.

Young Grant a Cadet at West Point—An Interesting Account of His Life at that Institution.

Young Grant entered the Military Academy at West Point in June, 1838. His first experience in martial life was in the licensed squad-drill to which the "pleb" is subjected by the remorseless company officers of the cadet battalion, and in the unlicensed "hazing" with which the new recruit is ruthlessly disciplined during his first season in camp.

At early dawn he is marched to and fro with the awkward squad over that famous plateau, to monotonous "One, two—one, two," which so frequently breaks in upon the morning nap of the guest at "Roe's;" and he may esteem himself fortunate if he is not rushed up the rugged road to Fort Putnam, at double-quick, on an empty stomach. When drill is dismissed, he betakes himself, with assumed composure, but with real anxiety, to the ambushes, surprises, flank movements, attacks in front and rear, which the senior cadets are preparing for him in the camp.

Life at West Point, though attractive in its mere external aspects, is still more so in its internal relations to the mind and character of the national ward. He learns there self-control and obedience, which are no despicable attainments, either for the man or the soldier. With a course of study so difficult that it tasks all the strength, and so varied that it addresses every faculty of the mind, the student has only to be faithful to himself and his opportunities, and he may acquire that extreme degree of mental control

which enables its fortunate possessor to turn the whole force and volume of his intellect, with equal facility, upon any subject and in any direction. Self-sacrificing patriotism is imbibed in the atmosphere, and fostered by all the associations, of the national school ; and the genius of the place, its history, trophies, mementoes, fire the spirit, and magnetize the soul.

The daily routine of cadet-life is somewhat monotonous. Drill and study are the accustomed order, relieved only by the evening dress parade, the inviting ramble through scenery charming alike by natural beauty and historic interest, the "Board of Visitors," annual encampments, graduations, and hops.

Martial law governs this military post ; and it is an efficient curb upon habits of irregularity and dissipation. Temperance and continence, within its jurisdiction, forfeit their place as virtues; for they are enforced upon the young soldier by inexorable necessity. Even a stolen visit to Benny Havens, a rollicking song by stealth, the smuggling in per steamer of contraband packages, under the pains and penalties of a court-martial, are too excruciating substitutes for genuine sport to be very seductive.

Grant encounters the severe exactions of the West Point course with no preparatory education worthy of the name. "Hasten slowly" was written on his forehead early in life; and those who knew him best expected from him a persistent rather than a brilliant scholarship in the intellectual exercises of the institution, and decided superiority only in the practical departments of military instruction. Both expectations were justified by his career as a cadet.

Abstract mathematics, topographical engineering, and the science of war, were conquered by his characteristic tenacity of will. Practical engineering succumbed with less difficulty; while infantry, artillery, and cavalry tactics were easily mastered.

He passed with *eclat* that "bridge of sighs," the first examination, and all the subsequent ones with no dishonor; earning successively the rank of corporal, sergeant, and commissioned officer of cadets. It is no small test, both of physical and mental prowers, to graduate at West Point. Feeble intellects yield to the severity of the studies, and feeble bodies to the hardships of the drill. Genuine attainment only can stand the searching ordeal of its four annual examinations; and the rules and regulations in regard to deportment and behavior are so trying to the careless buoyancy and undisciplined spirit of youth, that a diploma upon any terms should be regarded, not as a mere ovation, but a triumph.

When we consider that the untutored boy from the woods sustained himself in every trial of a class from which seventy were dropped; that he attained to the rank of twenty-one in a graduating class of thirty-nine, thus distancing threescore and ten who entered the race, and winning over eighteen who finally came to the goal; when we consider, also, that he never lost position or forfeited class-rank by demerits, we must yield to him the credit of more than ordinary capacity and subordination. Of how few who have entered West Point can so much be said!

The first order which issues to the graduating cadet may send him to some embryo territory in the West, and impose upon him at once the important duties of civil administration; or it may despatch him to the frontiers, within cannon-shot of a foreign flag, where he may be called to adjudicate, upon principles of public law, the perplexing questions which frequently arise between contiguous powers.

During his career as an officer, he can hardly escape

being placed in such relations. To prepare him for the intelligent discharge of these important positions is no insignificant part of the West Point course. He is, therefore, taught French as the language of diplomatic intercourse, and Spanish as the tongue of our Mexican neighbors. He is indoctrinated in the laws of nations, the jurisprudence of the United States, and the principles of municipal law. He is made as familiar with the authoritative commentaries of Kent and Wheaton's "International Code" as with Mahan's "Field Fortification" and Benton's "Course of Ordnance and Gunnery."

It is an error to suppose that our future officers are instructed only in what pertains to war as a theory and an art. Their preparation for civil affairs is as thorough and complete as that of the student in our colleges, or the lawyer in our towns. With sapping, mining, mortar-practice, and tactics for garrison and siege, are blended the logical rules and theories by which truth is eliminated and sophistries detected. With the science of war, which desolates, is interwoven the science of morals, which renovates and ameliorates the world.

Not only chemistry, which especially relates to fabricating the *materiel* of war, is embraced in its course of study, but astronomy, mechanics, physics, mineralogy, and the philosophy of history.

With a head stuffed with the learning of the school; with ambition kindled, and patriotism exalted, by the genius of the place; with a mind skilled to manœuvre, attack, and defend; a hand adroit in piling up redoubts and stockades, and in digging rifle-pits and intrenchments, and apt in constructing fascines, hurdles, and sap rollers; with all his sensibilities vivid, all his senses keen, intent, animated, the model of physical power and activity—Cadet Grant is launched into the stormy ocean of life.

Anecdote of Grant at West Point.

The following incident occurred while young Grant was serving his first year as a cadet of the Military Academy at West Point, and is a very good illustration of the coolness of his disposition.

It is related by his father in his interesting reminiscences of the early life of his distinguished son, published in the *New York Ledger*.

"As is well known, it is the practice at West Point to get some rig, run, or joke on every new comer. Ulysses took a letter of introduction to a cadet, who told him all this, and put him on his guard. In the course of the first night, one of the cadets, dressed as an officer, entered the room where Ulysses and his chum were sleeping, and told them that one of the rules of the institution required that a task should be given them, to see how they would get through it, while laboring under the excitement consequent upon their first admission. He then, producing a book, ordered that, before morning, they should each commit to memory a lesson of twenty pages. 'All right, all right,' responded Ulysses; and as soon as the pretended officer had withdrawn, he went quietly back to bed, while his companion sat up and studied all night. Of course, the recitation has not yet been called for."

Grant's career at West Point was uneventful, his demerits, as his father says, being mostly "of a trivial character, such as not having his coat buttoned, or his shoes tied right, or something of that kind." His progress was of the slow and sure kind ; holding firmly on to all he acquired, but having nothing of that dashing brilliancy which is thought so much of by collegiates. He did not, like many, only study to pass the examiner, and then forget what he had learned. Even if his seat was below those of some others in his classes, at the end of each year it would be found that his education was of a far more solid and substantial nature than that of several of his class-mates who stood higher in grades. Experience, however, has demonstrated that the rank attained at a Military Academy, or at college, affords a very uncertain indication of the future success or usefulness of *the man*.

What a Fellow Comrade Says of Young Grant at West Point —A Splendid Record.

A gentleman who was a comrade of young Grant for two years at West Point Military Academy, says :

I remember Grant as a plain, common-sense, straightforward youth; quiet, calm, thoughtful, and unaggressive; shunning notoriety; quite contented, while others were grumbling; taking to his military duties in a very businesslike manner; not a prominent man in the corps, but respected by all, and very popular with his friends. His sobriquet of *Uncle Sam* was given to him there, where every good-fellow has a nickname, from these very qualities; indeed, he was a very uncle-like sort of a youth.

He was then and always an excellent horseman, and his picture rises before me as I write, in the old torn coat (riding-jackets, if we remember rightly, had not then been issued, and the cadets always wore their seediest rig into the sweat and dust of the riding drill), obsolescent leather gig-top, loose riding pantaloons, with spurs buckled over them, going with his clanking sabre to the drill-hall. He exhibited but little enthusiasm in any thing; his best standing was in the mathematical branches, and their application to tactics and military engineering.

If we again dwell upon the fact that no one, even of his most intimate friends, dreamed of a great future for him, it is to add that, looking back now, we must confess that

EXAMINATION AT WEST POINT.

the possession of many excellent qualities, and the entire absence of all low and mean ones, establish a logical sequence from first to last, and illustrate, in a novel manner, the poet's fancy about—

> "The baby figures of the giant mass
> Of things to come at large,"

the germs of those qualities which are found in beautiful combination in Wordsworth's "Happy Warrior:"

> "The generous spirit who, when brought
> Among the tasks of real life, hath wrought
> Upon the plan that pleased his infant thought."

And at this point of view, as we find the Western boy, after the compacting, instructing, developing processes of West Point, coming forth a man, ready for the stern realities of American life, we may pause to point him out to our American youth as an example henceforth to be followed; then, as now, a character which, in the words of a friend, " betrayed no trust, falsified no word, violated no rights, manifested no tyranny, sought no personal aggrandizement, complained of no hardship, displayed no jealousy, oppressed no subordinate; but in whatever sphere, protected every interest, upheld his flag, and was ever known by his humanity, sagacity, courage, and honor."

What more can be claimed of any young man?

General Grant's Class-mates at West Point — Who They Were, and What They Have Done—An Interesting Biographical Series.

General Grant graduated at West Point the twenty-first in his class, June 30, 1843, with thirty-nine class-mates. The grade and brief biography of each is as follows:

The cadet who stood first in the class was William Benjamin Franklin, who entered the Topographical Engineer Corps; and having passed through a series of adventures under various commanders was, at the beginning of 1864, the general commanding the Nineteenth Army Corps, in the Department of the Gulf, under General Banks.

The names of the next three graduates do not now appear in the Army List of the United States.

Wm. F. Raynolds ranked fifth in the class, entered the infantry service, and was appointed an *aide* on the staff of General Fremont, commanding the Mountain Department, with the rank of colonel, from the 31st of March, 1862.

The next graduate was Isaac F. Quinby. He had entered the artillery service, and had been professor at West Point, but had retired to civil life. The rebellion, however, brought him from his retirement, and he went to the field at the head of a regiment of New York volunteers. He afterward became a brigadier-general in the Army of the Potomac.

Roswell S. Ripley, the author of "The War with Mexico," stood seventh; but his name does not now appear in the official Army Register of the United States, as he had attached himself to the rebel cause.

The next graduate was John James Peck, who entered the artillery service, and was, on January 1, 1864, the commander of the district of and army in North Carolina, which then formed a portion of General Butler's Department.

John P. Johnstone, the daring artillery lieutenant who fell gallantly at Contreras, Mexico, was the next graduate.

General Joseph Jones Reynolds was the next in grade. This officer had gained great credit, while in the army, as a professor of sciences, but had resigned some time when the rebellion broke out. He was, however, in 1861, again brought forward as a general of three-months volunteers, under General McClellan, in Western Virginia; was afterward commissioned by the President; and latterly became attached to the Army of the Cumberland. He served on the staff of the general commanding that army, with the rank of major-general, until General Grant assumed command of the military division embracing the Departments of Ohio, Tennessee, and Cumberland, when he was transferred to New Orleans.

The eleventh graduate was James Allen Hardie, who, during the War of the Rebellion, became an Assistant Adjutant-General of the Army of the Potomac, with the rank of colonel.

Henry F. Clarke stood twelfth, entered the artillery service, gained brevets in Mexico, and became chief commissary of the Army of the Potomac, during the War of the Rebellion, with the rank of colonel.

Lieutenant Booker, the next in grade, died while in service at San Antonio, Texas, on June 26, 1849.

The fourteenth graduate might have been a prominent officer of the United States Army, had he not deserted the cause of his country, and attached himself to the rebels. He had not even the excuse of " going with his State," for he was a native of New Jersey, and was appointed to the army from that State. His name is Samuel G. French, major-general of the rebel army.

The next graduate was Lieutenant Theodore L. Chadbourne, who was killed at the battle of Resaca de la Palma, on May 9, 1846, after distinguishing himself for his bravery at the head of his command.

Christopher Colon Augur, one of the commanders of the Department of Washington, and major-general of volunteers, was the next in grade.

We now come to another renegade. Franklin Gardner, a native of New York, and an appointee from the State of Iowa, graduated seventeenth in General Grant's class. At the time of the rebellion he deserted the cause of the United States and joined the rebels. He was disgracefully dropped from the rolls of the United States Army, on May 7, 1861, became a major-general in the rebel service, and had to surrender his garrison at Port Hudson, July 9, 1863, through the reduction of Vicksburg by his junior graduate, U. S. Grant.

Lieutenant George Stevens, who was drowned in the passage of the Rio Grande, May 18, 1846, was the next graduate.

The nineteenth graduate was Edmund B. Holloway, of Kentucky, who obtained a brevet at Contreras, and was a captain of infantry in the United States regular army at the commencement of the rebellion. Although his State remained in the Union, he threw up his commission on May 14, 1861, and joined the rebels.

The graduate that immediately preceded General Grant was Lieutenant Lewis Neill, who died on January 13, 1850, while in service at Fort Croghan, Texas.

GENERAL GRANT was the twenty-first graduate.

Joseph H. Potter, of New Hampshire, graduated next after the hero of Vicksburg. During the War of the Rebellion he became a colonel of volunteers, retaining his rank as captain in the regular army.

Lieutenant Robert Hazlitt, who was killed in the storming of Monterey, September 21, 1846, and Lieutenant Edwin Howe, who died while in service at Fort Leavenworth, March 31, 1850, were the next two graduates.

Lafayette Boyer Wood, of Virginia, was the twenty-fifth graduate. He is no longer connected with the service, having resigned several years before the rebellion.

The next graduate was Charles S. Hamilton who, for some time commanded, as major-general of volunteers, a district under General Grant, who at that time was chief of the Department of the Tennessee.

Captain William K. Van Bokkelen, of New York, who was cashiered for rebel proclivities, on May 8, 1861, was the next graduate, and was followed by Alfred St. Amand Crozet, of New York, who had resigned the service several years before the breaking out of the civil war, and Lieutenant Charles E. James, who died at Sonoma, Cal., on June 8, 1849.

The thirtieth graduate was the gallant General Frederick Steele, who participated in the Vicksburg and Mississippi campaigns, as division and corps commander under General Grant, and afterward commanded the Army of Arkansas.

The next graduate was Captain Henry R. Selden, of Vermont, and of the Fifth U. S. Infantry.

General Rufus Ingalls, quartermaster-general of the Army of the Potomac, graduated No. 32, and entered the mounted rifle regiment, but was found more valuable in the Quartermaster's Department, in which he held the rank of major from January 12, 1862, with a local rank of brigadier-general of volunteers from May 23, 1863.

Major Frederick T. Dent, of the Fourth U. S. Infantry, and Major J. C. McFerran, of the Quartermaster's Department, were the next two graduates.

The thirty-fifth graduate was General Henry Moses Judah, who commanded a division of the Twenty-Third

Army Corps during its operations after the rebel cavalry general, John H. Morgan, and in East Tennessee, during the fall of 1863.

The remaining four graduates were Norman Elting, who resigned the service October 29, 1846; Cave J. Couts, who was a member of the State Constitutional Convention of California during the year 1849; Charles G. Merchant, of New York; and George C. McClelland, of Pennsylvania, no one of whom is now connected with the United States Service.

It is very interesting to look over the above list to see how the twenty-first graduate has outstripped all his seniors in grade, showing plainly that true talent will ultimately make its way, no matter how modest the possessor may be, and notwithstanding all the opposition that may be placed in its way by others. It will be seen how General Grant came to command a larger force and a greater extent of country than all his thirty-eight class-mates put together, and has risen higher in the military scale than any in his class, notwithstanding the fact that he did not seem to possess the same amount of apparent dashing ability.

His Scotch blood, however, gave him a pertinacity of character that enabled him to push forward against all difficulties, and this stubborn perseverance even in the midst of disappointments has characterized the whole of his life, civil, military and executive. When, however, he found he was on the right track he kept to it without turning aside for even a moment, and so ultimately became successful.

IN MEXICO.

General Grant's First Battle — Called From the Swamps of Louisiana to the Plains of Mexico — At Palo Alto and Resaca — Leaping Into the "Ravine of Palms" — His Grand Bayonet Charge.

Grant was full second lieutenant and still attached to the Fourth Infantry when the order reached him—in the remote swamps of Louisiana—"to join the army of occupation at Corpus Christi." He had been initiated in all the theories of war, cruel arts and mysteries at West Point. He had conned her entangling maxims, and tracked her crimson footsteps over the desolated earth; with maps and plans before him, and with critical eye he had surveyed her renowned Aceldemas; he had, as part of his daily task, analyzed her infernal ingenuity in concentrating and scattering armies; and, before models of her most formidable strongholds, had sat down as a besieger, and approached, stormed, and captured them. Through Jomini's animated pages he had marched, counter-marched, and halted at points of vantage; drawn up and extended lines of battle; flanked, and pierced the centre; and charged, vanquished, and pursued—with Frederick and Napoleon. He had almost seen War in vision, and toyed with her snaky locks, and played with her thunder-bolts. Like a votary of the black-art, he felt an irresistible impulse to utter the cabalistic spell which should usher him into the visible presence of the demon. In a word, he had the natural inclination of all men who have mastered theories to apply their principles to practice.

TROPICAL CLIMES.

War was now waving her torch along our frontiers. The surcharged clouds were lowering on the southwestern horizon. Her birds of ill-omen, snuffing the carnage afar, were gathering in from every side. Lines of bristling bayonets were confronting each other on opposite banks of the Rio Grande.

He marched with the army, March 8, 1846, to Fort Brown, and " flashed the sword," which the Government had taught him to wield when Ringold's battery first struck the staggering line of Mexicans in that prairie-thicket which gives to the earliest action in the Mexican war its name.

When, on the next day, the stricken, but undemoralized enemy rallied reinforcements on a stronger position, and it became apparent, as the sun was declining, that cannon could not, as on the previous day, decide the contest, Lieutenant Grant was deployed as a skirmisher, with his regimental comrades, towards the natural ditch in which the foe was intrenched; and he was on the lead when the gallant Fourth leaped into the " ravine of palms" *and cleared it of every hostile bayonet!*

When the Mexicans rallied again, Grant charged with that unwavering line of steel, which finally broke them into fragments and scattered them on the river. This occurred May 9, 1846.

On the 18th of the same month, Grant crossed the Rubicon—that is the Rio Grande—and occupied Matamoras with General Taylor's column, while the haggard and sullen remnant of the hostile army was creeping slowly southward.

IN MEXICO.

General Grant's First "Baptism in Blood"—The American Columns Torn to Pieces before Fort Teneria—Tunnelling Walls and Fighting on Roofs of Houses—Grant "Foremost in the Ranks."

On the 20th of August, 1846, Grant finds himself on that abrupt eminence which commands a prospect of Monterey from the east. At his feet lies a cultivated valley, tessellated with the varied green and yellow of orange and acacia groves, and waving fields of corn and sugar-cane, which stretch up to the very bastions of the easternmost works of defense. Beyond the forts, the sunbeams glance on the marble-like stucco of the cathedral and dwellings of the city, which seems to be veiled even from the profane gaze of the northern barbarians by the luxuriant foliage of flowering tropical trees.

Behind all, rise heavenward the Saddle and Mitre Mountains with their tremendous peaks, abruptly compared to "giants guarding the lovely bower at their feet and prepared to roll enormous rocks from their summits upon the adventurous assailants."

The morning of the 21st breaks clear and resplendent; and Major Mansfield, who is in the front, reconnoitreing, sends back word that he has discovered a point where that foremost fortification—Fort Teneria—is assailable.

In a moment Colonel Garland, with two infantry regiments, Bragg's battery, and the Baltimore battalion, is descending the slope, followed by the rapt attention and palpitating hearts of their comrades on the hill.

Before they had reached the point designated by Mansfield, the citadel enfilades them with its fire, and a masked battery in front showers them with shot and shell. Fort Teneria meantime is silent but frowns like grim death. On they advance, until they can see the eyes of the gunners, when, presto, the fort opens, and the assailing American columns, torn to pieces, are hurled into the suburbs of the city, to be massacred piecemeal by musketry from walls and housetops.

Meanwhile the Fourth Infantry, to which Grant was attached, had been ordered to march by the left flank towards the point of attack; but ignorant of the fate of their comrades, they moved directly against the fort, when the same destructive fire sweeps from the earth two thirds of their number, and scatters the survivors in dismay.

Fortunately for the success of the day, two companies of Colonel Garland's discomfited storming-party find shelter on the roof of a tannery, within musket-range of Teneria, and, with the sure aim of the rested rifle, pick off, one by one, the Mexican gunners. Under the cover of repeated and overwhelming volleys from this "coigne of vantage," the Tennessee and Mississippi volunteers rush across an intervening space of a hundred yards, and, with a deafening war-whoop, pour like angry billows up the slope, over the parapet and through the embrasure.

The work at the east end is over for the day, and the Fourth Infantry bivouac in Teneria for the night. We have been thus particular in detailing this affair, because it was Grant's first encounter with war "in all its terrors clad" and because, from his experience there in both of its vicissitudes, and from its frightful slaughter, it may be said to have terminated his martial novitiate by a "baptism of blood."

Grant discovers at morning *reveille*, that Fort Diablo has been evacuated during the night, and is now occupied by the Mississippi Volunteers; and the cheering news reaches him at breakfast, that General Worth, by a succession of impetuous assaults, has carried every fortified position on the western acclivities. The guns of the Bishop's Palace are now turned upon the devoted town from the west, and those of Teneria and Diablo from the east; and, simultaneously from each of these directions, the riflemen are penetrating the suburbs, and gradually each other and the central plaza.

The assailants find every street barricaded with masonwork, every wall pierced for musketry, and on every second roof a sand-bag battery. Crawling from roof to roof, burrowing from house to house, literally tunneling covered ways through the solid walls of the dwellings, the sharpshooters, from opposite directions have arrived within four blocks of each other; and between the two, huddled around the Cathedral, is the Mexican garrison.

This Cathedral is the Mexican powder magazine and the shells that Major Monroe now and then lets fall within close and amazingly dangerous proximity soon called out the bugle blast and flag of truce, and on the 24th of September, Ampudia capitulates.

Gen. Grant's First Siege — He Personally Supervises Twelve Miles of Trench and Parallel, from which he Shatters the Enemy's Redoubts and Bastions.

The siege of Vera Cruz, though of short duration, illustrated many of the most important principles of engineering.

It was the first siege in which Lieut. Grant had any experience. He personally supervised the construction of those twelve miles of trench and parallel, bristling with eighty-nine batteries; that circle within a circle of constantly advancing fire, which, day after day, closed in nearer and nearer on wailing Vicksburg, until it was slowly strangled by coils which it was impotent either to sever or endure—the first of a soldier who afterwards environed Richmond with ramparts even more Titan-like and irresistible; bisecting the area of treason by the one triumph, and by the other exterminating rebellion and destroying the confederacy.

The first parallel at Vera Cruz was drawn at a distance of eleven hundred yards, from which a battery of three thirty-two pounders, and as many Paixhans, finally succeeded in demolishing the curtain, and shattering the redoubts and bastions and destroying half the houses on the land side. The bombs of the mortar batteries burned up all the combustible houses.

The flag of truce appeared on the third day; and negotiations were opened, which terminated in the surrender of Vera Cruz and San Juan d' Ulloa. The capture of those strongly-fortified points will always be memorable as the first siege in which General Grant so signally and ably participated.

General Grant's First Official Compliments as a Soldier — The First "Brevet."

Grant was favorably noticed for his skill in gunnery, when that cordon of earthworks was tightening round Vera Cruz—the "Invincible." He was complimented for his gallantry at Cherubusco, when the *tete de pont* was carried by the bayonet alone.

He won his brevet of " First Lieutenant " in those bloody hours when Molino Del Rey succumbed to the impetuosity of the United States soldiery; and the full grade on that day, ever memorable in our annals, when the steep and frowning heights of Chapultepec were carried, and the trembling city below implored the mercy of our artillery.

In Capt. Brooks' report of the operations of the Second Artillery against Chapultepec, the following paragraph occurs:

"I succeeded in reaching the fort with a few men. Here Lieut. U. S. Grant and a few more men of the Fourth Infantry, found me; and by a joint movement, after an obstinate resistance, a strong field-work was carried, and the enemy's right was completely turned."

Major Lee, in his report of operations against the same fortress, mentions the same officer in the following strain:

"At the first barrier, the enemy was in strong force, which rendered it necessary to advance with caution. This was done; and, when the head of the battalion was within short musket-range of the barrier, Lieut. Grant, Fourth Infantry, and Capt. Brooks, Second Artillery, with a few men of their respective regiments, by a handsome movement to the left, turned the right flank of the enemy, and the barrier was carried. Lieut. Grant behaved with distinguished gallantry on the 13th and 14th."

The following passage occurs in Col. Garland's report of the same action: " The rear of the enemy had made a stand behind a breastwork, from which they were driven by detachments of the Second Artillery under Capt. Brooks, and the Fourth Infantry under Lieut. Grant, supported by other regiments of the division, after a short, sharp conflict. I recognized the command as it came up, mounted a howitzer on the top of a convent, which, under the direction of Lieut. Grant, Quartermaster of the Fourth Infantry, and Lieut. Lendrum, Third Artillery, annoyed the enemy considerably. I must not omit to call attention to Lieut. Grant, who acquitted himself most nobly upon several occasions under my observation."

"I have again to make acknowledgments to Cols. Garland and Clarke, brigade commanders, as also to their respective staffs; to S. Smith, Haller, and *Grant*, Fourth Infantry, especially."—*Gen. Worth's Report of Battle of Chapultepec.*

The First "Flank Movement"—An Opposing Army Which Grant Thought Best to Pass Around, With Heavy Margins, to "the Left"—Scaling the Heights of Cerro Gordo.

Where the national road crosses the Rio del Plan, you instantly rise from the *tierra caliente* into a more elevated region, and, after an hour's march, stand at the entrance of one of the defiles, so famous in war-like story, which Liberty, loving the mountains, gives to mountaineers for their defense.

Here, on the left, rises a ridge, extending the whole length of the pass, and behind it rolls the rapid but shallow river through a cañon a hundred feet in depth. Upon its acclivities, facing the road and in advantageous positions, the Mexicans have planted their heavy batteries, one above the other; and the superior commands all the aproaches to the inferior.

Here, on your right, are elongated mountain spurs, basing upon the road their slopes, covered with impenetrable chaparral. They forbid any diversion to the right.

Still farther west, and in the direct line of your march, stand two conical mounts—Atalaya, masked from the road by one of the spurs; and Cerro Gordo, lifting itself eight hundred feet above the plain, and presenting to you an eastern face, steep, rugged, difficult of access, and strengthened, moreover, by two tiers of breastworks and abatis. Its summit is crowned by a tower, mounting nine guns, which sweep the defile and the road beyond it.

As if this were not enough to guard the pass at the foot of Cerro Gordo, a battery of six guns is planted directly on the road. You can not find, in any direction, a half acre of level earth, where a battalion can deploy, which is not commanded by artillery.

Grant sees in an instant that here is no merely engineer-

SUMMIT OF POPOCATAPETL.

"The numerous steeples, of great beauty and elevation, with Popocatapetl ten thousand feet higher, apparently near enough to touch with the hand, filled the mind with religious awe. Recovering from the sublime trance, probably not a man in the column failed to say to his neighbor or himself, "*That splendid city soon shall be ours!*"

(*Scott's Aut biography.*)

ing question, but a *complex problem in the art of war*, which addresses itself to the highest genius of the commander. It needs but a glance *at his left* to show him that no skill and courage can turn the enemy's right. To the left of his line alone a *flanking movement* can be aimed. And here on his right are these entangled spurs; and the resources of reconnoissance have been tasked in vain to find a pathway through them.

Shall the army be sacrificed in forcing the defile ? Shall it be decimated in storming the fort? Shall the expedition be abandoned ?

When Scott reaches the ground, his experienced eye speedily detects the sole expedient which can brush this great obstruction from his path. Let Pillow's brigade seriously threaten, and if practicable carry, these batteries of the enemy on the left of the road. Let Twiggs' division, before it reaches the defile, wheel sharp to the right into this forest of chaparral, and cutting a pathway behind those elongated ridges, and encircling all the Mexican works, debouch beyond them all into the national road.

Assail Cerro Gordo, the key of the whole position, in the rear; and at the same time cut off the retreat of the enemy to Jalapa. This was Scott's preliminary order of battle, omitting only his directions to the artillery and cavalry reserve, to Worth—to follow and support the operations of Twiggs, and the directions for the vigorous pursuit of the foe after his intrenchments were carried.

The performance corresponds with the programme, except that Twiggs, being annoyed by a party of skirmishers in executing his movement, throws off to his left a detachment to scatter them, which unexpectedly carries the cone-shaped Atalaya, and, encouraged thereby, scales Cerro Gordo in front, and turns to flight one division of

Santa Anna's Mexican army before Twiggs' right, on the march, has reached the Jalapa Road to intercept it.

Such was Grant's *first participation in a flanking movement.*

There was another man in this army who might be mentioned in this connection, and whom General Grant, long years afterwards, met under peculiar circumstances. It was Robert E. Lee, then serving on General Scott's staff as captain of engineers.

General Grant's First Half Year of War—It Opens on Fields of Sublimest Imagery, but they are Storied in Human Sacrifice and Midnight Superstitions — Grant Amid Pyramids, Smoking Mountains, and on the Heights of Chapultepec.

Grant's first half year of war was one of peculiar enchantment.

War assumed her most comely guise, her most captivating airs, her most bewitching smile, and wove round the entranced young warrior all her fascinating spells.

It is hard to conceive, it is impossible to describe, the exhilaration with which he participated in that series of hard-fought engagements which bore triumphantly the flag of the young Republic from the shores of the Gulf to the lake-encircled metropolis of the ancient Aztecs, in the footprints of previous conquerors, whose names recalled the palmiest days of the proudest monarchy; through scenery grand and picturesque beyond all example; along the base of volcanoes once crowned with fire, now lifting eternal snow far into the azure depths of air; amid the ruins of temples which once smoked with human sacrifice; and along the majestic front of colossal pyramids, which carry the mind back to a primeval race and an extinct civilization.

General Scott, who visited the Pyramid of Cholula, thus describes it:

" During his halt, every corps of the army, in succession, made a most interesting excursion of six miles to the ruins of the ancient City of Cholula, long, in point of civilization

THE PYRAMID OF CHOLULA.

and art, the Etruria of this continent, and, in respect to religion, the Mecca of many of the earliest tribes known to tradition.

"One grand feature, denoting the ancient grandeur of Cholula, stands but little affected by the lapse of, perhaps, thousands of years—a pyramid built of alternate layers of brick and clay, some two hundred feet in height, with a square basis of more than forty acres, running up to a plateau of seventy yards square. There stood, in the time of Cortez, the great pagan temple of the Cholulans, with a perpetual blazing fire on its altar, seen in the night many miles around.

"Coming up with the brigade, marching at ease, all intoxicated with the fine air and splendid scenery, he (General Scott) was, as usual, received with hearty and protracted cheers. The group of officers who surrounded him differed widely in their objects of admiration; some preferring this or that snow-capped mountain, others the city, and some the Pyramid of Cholula, that was now opening upon the view."

Prescott says: "The great *Volcan*, as Popocatapetl was called, rose to the enormous height of 17,852 feet above the level of the sea—more than 2,000 feet above the 'monarch of the mountains,' the highest elevation in Europe. During the present century it has rarely given evidence of its volcanic origin; and the 'hill that smokes' has almost forfeited its claim to the appellation. But at the time of the Conquest it was frequently in a state of activity, and raged with uncommon fury while the Spaniards were at Tiascala.'

"On they trudged, however, stopping now and then to quench their thirst at some mountain brook, or to gaze at the quenched volcano of Popocatapetl, its sides begrimed with lava, and its peak soaring above the clouds."—*Scott's Battles in Mexico.*

Of Cholula, Prescott says: "It was of great antiquity, and was founded by the primitive races that overspread the land before the Aztecs.

"The Mexican temples—*teocallis*, 'houses of God' as they were called—were very numerous.

"Human sacrifices were adopted by the Aztecs early in the fourteenth century, about two hundred years before the Conquest."—*Prescott's Conquest of Mexico.*

Nor was it any drawback to his enjoyment, that, with every step of this exciting campaign, Lieutenant Grant was advancing in military knowledge and capacity, and also in professional reputation and rank.

He was favorably noticed for his skill in gunnery, when that cordon of earthworks was tightening round Vera Cruz, the " Invincible."

He was complimented for his gallantry at Churubusco, when the *tete de pont* was carried by the bayonet alone.

He won his brevet of first lieutenant in those bloody hours when Molino Del Rey succumbed to the impetuosity of our soldiery; and the full grade on that day, ever memorable in our annals, when the steep and frowning heights of Chapultepec were carried and the trembling city below implored the mercy of our victorious soldiery.

IN MEXICO.

On to Mexico—Grant's First Experience in Capturing a Capital—A Great and Glittering City Approached by the High-ways of Death—Grant's Active Part in the Dreadful Struggle.

The general of the division under whom it was Grant's good fortune to serve, was Scott's right arm during the Mexican campaign: wherever hard work was to be done, Worth was in the van. Garland and Clarke were the right and left arms of Worth. Of Col. Garland, Worth himself says, that "he was conspicuous on many fields of the Mexican War; and by his skill, conduct, and courage in the last great combats, greatly added to an already established reputation for patriotism and soldiership."

In following closely Col. Garland's impeded march to the capital, we shall detect the "whereabouts" of Lieut. Grant in the smoke of the battle, and shall witness "the moving accidents by flood and field, disastrous chances, hair-breadth 'scapes i' the imminent deadly breach," through which Grant himself reached his "first environed capital"—the Hall of the Montezumas.

He was at this time quartermaster of the Fourth, and unless called to service upon the regimental staff, might have remained with his baggage-wagons during every engagement; but he coveted no such exemption, and was always foremost in its fighting ranks.

We know, then, that on this bright forenoon in September—it is the 20th of the month, 1844—Grant was standing with his brigade-comrades in an angle of the San Antonio Causeway. They propose by this route to make an excursion to the City of Mexico, and enter it by the San Antonio Gate.

They possess some exciting information which it is desirable that the reader shall also learn in order to enter into the spirit of their adventure. They know that some opposition is to be anticipated to their jaunt.

They can see that, half a mile ahead, the villagers of San Antonio have thrown impediments across the causeway which may prematurely arrest their project. They know that Col. Clarke, with their co-brigade, who designs to accompany them, has already diverged into the meadows for the purpose of avoiding the intended civilities of this *hacienda*, and reaching the road at a point beyond it.

They know that some three miles ahead, where this causeway crosses the Churubusco rivulet, still more formal preparations are made for their reception; that a *tete de pont* has been erected with bastions, connecting-curtains, wet ditch, everything in the most approved engineering style and finish, even to the four guns in embrasure and barbette, bearing directly upon their narrow path; and that, if the Mexicans having them in charge are mischievously disposed, quite serious consequences may there ensue.

They know that a breastwork of some four hundred yards front connects this *tete de pont* with the convent church of San Pablo, in the hamlet of Churubusco; and that, strange to say, a redoubt and abatis obstructs the entrance into the sacred edifice, which, moreover, mounts seven cannon on its consecrated walls, crenelled also for musketry.

They know, also, that Santa Anna, with a following of twenty-seven thousand soldiers, has come forth from his palace to this interesting locality for the purpose of greeting them upon their arrival.

They know that beyond the river and the bridge some eight thousand Mexican reserves are drawn up in line, awaiting their advent. They know that yesterday morning General Twiggs, with quite a large retinue, went through

INTERIOR GREAT CATHEDRAL, CITY OF MEXICO.

the Pedregal, some five miles to the west, for the purpose of visiting the fortified camp of General Valencia, who, with a concourse of friends, has also emerged from the city with hospitable intent.

They know that it is the plan of General Twiggs' party, after paying their respects to the Mexican general, to pursue a circuitous path for the purpose of avoiding the parade and ceremonies at Churubusco, and to join Garland beyond the river in his excursion to the city.

Grant, with the brigade, is awaiting the signal which shall announce that Clarke has reached his point of destination. His guns at length are heard.

Garland's war-dogs, unleashed, rush impetuously upon the San Antonio intrenchments, and drive out the enemy in a long straggling column, which Clarke, now charging from the meadows on its flank, cuts near the centre, hurling the rear upon the village of Dolores as unworthy of further notice, but uniting with Garland in scourging the severed head to the compatriot embrace of Churubusco. But the Sixth Infantry, which is on the lead, suddenly comes to a halt.

The battle rages at three points at once. Victory wavers, and it is doubtful upon which banner she will perch. Garland's and Clarke's brigades are stunned in their onslaught upon the flank of the *tete de pont*. The veteran Sixth Infantry stagger back, decimated from their furious leap upon its front.

Duncan's battery is obliged to mask itself before the heavier metal of its guns. Taylor's battery, operating with Twiggs upon the right, crippled in men and horses, is driven from its position by the expert gunnery of San Pablo, while the assailing infantry there are terribly galled by the sharpshooters of its tower and roof, and Shields on the meadows is outflanked by the Mexican cavalry.

One daring exploit redeems the fortunes of the day—
Lieut. Longstreet, bearing the colors of the Eighth Infantry, and leading the regiment which he inspirits both by exhortation and example, leaps with it into the dry-ditch of the *tete de pont*, escalades the curtain without ladder or scaling-implement, and, with the cold steel alone, clears its bastions of defenders, and drives them over the bridge upon their reserve. Quicker than thought, he turns its captured guns upon San Pablo, which is still slaughtering the columns of Twiggs upon the right.

Relieved from the pressure of the same metal, Lieut.-Col. Duncan gallops forward with his splendid battery. He opens at a distance of two hundred yards, upon the walls around the convent; and seizing the prolongation of its principal face, in the space of five minutes, by a fire of astonishing rapidity, drives the artillery-men from the guns in that quarter, and the infantry from their intrenchments; and then turns his battery upon the convent tower.

While its garrison are shocked and half demoralized by this overwhelming attack of Duncan from the left, the stormers upon the right capture the nearest salient which confronts them in that direction; the light artillery advance rapidly within effective range; San Pablo slackens fire; and a dozen white flags appear just as Capt. Alexander of the Third Infantry is entering it, sword in hand. The whole fortified position of Churubusco is taken.

It was yet dark on the following morning, when Grant, in regimental battle line, confronts the last fortified position upon which depends the fate of the enemy's capital. Directly in his front the solid walls of Molino del Rey, five hundred yards in length, rise like a precipice, save that drowsy candles twinkle through its windows, intimating what is in store when from them shall stare the muzzles of the rifles.

On its right the Casa Mata, or arsenal, presents a forbidding mass of heavy masonry, pierced for musketry, and enveloped by a quadrangular field-work. Between the two is the station of the enemy's field-battery and of the infantry deployed on either side for its protection. On its left, wrapped in the solemn shade of gigantic cypresses, towers from the summit of a porphyritic rock the royal castle of Chapultepec.

Casa Mata is assigned to Grant's comrades of the Second Brigade as their exclusive prey. Garland, under whom he serves, is aimed at the Molino alone, which, by the masking of Chapultepec, has become the extreme left of the enemy; and his business is threefold—to sustain Wright's storming party, to protect Huger's battery of twenty-four-pounders, to cut off supports from the castle.

The co-operating forces for the single movement in which Grant is personally concerned are all now in position. Garland is on the plain, staring directly into the eyes of the Molino; and on the Tacubaya ridge, within five hundred yards of it, Huger, with his matches lighted; Wright, with his forlorn hope in leash; Cadwallader and Kirby Smith, as reserves against mishaps—all with hearts kindled, muscles braced, teeth set, awaiting the opening of an exciting drama.

Morn has hardly purpled the east, before the heavy missiles of Huger's battering train pound the walls and penetrate the roof of the Molino; and, before the nearest mountain brings back the echo of his first gun, lights flash, bugles sound, shouts run, and arms clash along the whole line of the enemy's defenses, as the roused garrison begird themselves for action. At the first indication that the mason-work is yielding, Wright, with his half-legion of stormers, advances at double-quick down the Tacubaya slope; and unchecked by the ditch which environs the structure, unshaken by the sheet of flame which flashes from the light battery, by 'the musketry which showers upon them, by the canister and grape which enfilade every approach, in spite of its supports, captures the enemy's field-battery between the Casa Mata and the Molino.

But as they are trailing the guns upon the retreating mass, and before they are discharged, the garrison, perceiving that it has been dispossessed by a handful of men, and re-assured by the active support of its collateral lines, rallies in force, and temporarily discomfits and drives the victors. While they are bayoneting the wounded Americans left upon the field, Cadwallader's and Kirby Smith's reserves are on the assassins.

Garland now rapidly moves forward with Drum's section of artillery, and carries an apparently impregnable position under the guns of Chapultepec; and, stimulated by victory, wheels up his glittering line of bayonets to the support of the storming party. The Fourth joins the *melange* of all arms which have closed in upon the Molino, firing upon its apertures, climbing to its roof, and striving, with the butts of muskets and extemporized battering-rams, to burst its doors.

Major Buchanan of the Fourth, with Alden and Grant, are forcing the southern gate. Ayres and Anderson, with some dashing acrobats, vault through an embrasure at the northwest angle. A hand-to-hand fight ensues, from room to room, from floor to floor, from roof to roof. In the main apartment of the building, a stalwart Mexican gathers his straggling comrades into a line which threatens to clear the Molino of every assailant; but the southern gate has yielded, Buchanan and Grant appear with a serried file of the Fourth Infantry, and the Molino is finally captured beyond peradventure.

It is thus that Grant *wins his first brevet.* Before noon

the Casa Mata is blown up, the Molino dismantled, and the fatigued survivors of this desperate contest are reposing on their laurels at headquarters.

While these grand events are transpiring, Worth's division, stripped of its first brigade by Pillow's requisition, is awaiting at the Molino its predestined occupation. The order at length arrives; and Garland leads cautiously around the northern base of that consecrated hill under the sombre shade of its primeval grove, cheered by the stars and stripes which now flaunt defiance from turrets reared by Spanish viceroys, aimed at the entrance of the Causeway San Cosme, and bound for the Alameda by the northwestern gate. Grant is with him, and wins an additional grade on this immortal afternoon.

When they reach the embankment they perceive that it is no place for organized operations: it is narrow; the ubiquitous canals are on either side; an aqueduct runs along the center, laid on arches of solid masonry; it is intersected by numerous dikes and cross-roads and by frowning barricades, behind which the sullen enemy lies in wait. The brigade is broken into detachments: a part are thrown out, right and left, into the marsh, advancing behind every natural obstacle and cover; a part rush stealthily from arch to arch. Garland is now approaching the first breastwork. Behind it is the enemy in force, with his center resting upon it and his wings expanded.

"When the head of the battalion was in short musket-range of this barrier," writes Major Lee, commander of the Fourth, "Lieut. Grant and Capt. Brooks, with a few men of their respective regiments, by a handsome movement to the left, turned the right of the enemy, and the barrier was carried." The soldiers display their habitual firmness and audacity. Worth directs the movement with tactical exactness—massing his scattered detachments upon the enemy in front, while carefully guarding his own flank; throwing off artillery and infantry into the marsh upon the left to turn an abatis, into the marsh upon the right to clear his own and Quitman's front, who is pursuing a divergent march to the capital. Worth pushes his troops through a withering fire. They capture a second battery; they silence and dismantle a third, which enfilades their path. They have reached Campo Santo, where the causeway wheels into the inhabited streets of the city.

"We here came in front of another battery," writes General Worth in his report, "beyond which, distant some two hundred and fifty yards, and sustaining it, was the last defense, or the *garita* of San Cosme. The approach to these two defenses was in a right line; and the whole space was literally swept by grape, canister, and shells, from a heavy gun and howitzer; added to which, severe fires of musketry were delivered from the tops of the adjacent houses and churches.

It hence became necessary to vary our mode of operations. Garland's brigade was thrown to the right, within and masked by the aqueduct, and instructed to dislodge the enemy from the buildings in his front, and endeavor to reach and turn the left of the *garita;* taking advantage of such cover as might offer to enable him to effect these objects. Clarke's brigade was, at the same time, ordered to take the buildings on the left of the road, and, by the use of bars and picks, burrow through from house to house, and in like manner carry the right of the *garita*.

While these orders were being executed, a mountain howitzer was placed on the top of a commanding building on the left, and another on the Church of San Cosme on the right; both of which opened with admirable effect. The work of the troops was tedious, and necessarily slow, but was greatly favored by the fire of the howitzers." The howitzer on San Cosme Convent is served by a steady arm, and aimed by a sure eye, that will yet be of service to the country in direr extremities than this.

"I recognized the command as it came up," writes Col. Garland in his report of the action, "mounted a howitzer on the top of a convent, which, under the direction of Lieut. Grant, Quartermaster of the Fourth Infantry, and Lieut. Lendrum, Third Artillery, annoyed the enemy considerably. I must not omit to call attention to Lieut. Grant, who acquitted himself most nobly upon several occasions under my observation."

The orders which Worth recites in the paragraph we have transcribed from his report, virtually abrogates tactics for the remainder of the day, and transforms the movement into a hand-to-hand fight.

While Grant is showering the roofs with his howitzer, Garland is bush-fighting on one side of the street, and Clarke burrowing on the other.

And now ensues a scene which beggars description. The military vocabulary, with its technical terms, and the stereotyped phrases and imagery of military narrative, are powerless here. The sun is near the horizon. The war in the afternoon, with scope and verge enough, had, like a freshet, overspread the wide area of the meadows. It is now "bottled up" in a narrow gorge between the parallel walls of the street and the gate-works at its termination. The pent-up fury devours all before it; rages, howls, lashes the sides of the enclosure, as if a whole menagerie of rabid animals had been driven into a single pen.

By patient toil, ingenuity, courage unparalleled; by Clarke on the left, with his model cannoneers transmogrified into sappers and gymnasts; by Garland on the right, with his splendid infantry reduced for the occasion into bushwhackers; by Grant and Lendrum razeed into com-

TROPICAL GARDENS.

mon gunners; by cavalrymen dismounted, voltigeurs, engineers (for all arms are in this grand *melee*)—inch by inch, foot by foot, we crowd the Mexican gunners from the battery between us and the gateway. Duncan's artillery is rushed into the abandoned work with a velocity which drives it muzzle to muzzle against the enemy's cannon. "Once more to the breach!"

And by manœuvres which were never dreamed of on parade; by tactics which would astound the schools and dismay the martinet; by vaulting from house-top to house-top, squirming from window to window, worming from wall to wall; by soldiers right-face, left-face, back-face, obliqued; by soldiers erect, on their knees, "belly-whapper;" by volleys from cannon in the street, howitzers on the convent; by fusilades from all rifles, all muskets, all revolvers, from all skirmishers, squads, detachments, single men; by bullets from every loop-hole, cover, "coigne of vantage" —the riddled *garita* sullenly yields. The welkin rings with a shout which carries consternation to ten thousand Mexican homes, as the pent-up war went roaring through the pass. The city is ours!

Lieut. Grant Witnessing General Scott's Triumphal Entry into the City of Mexico—What He Sees from the Grand Plaza.

Grant was an interested spectator of that splendid pageant, the culminating felicity of Scott's long military career—his ceremonious entrance, with all the honors, into the City of Mexico.

He sees groups of discharged felons, wearing their tattered mantles with the air of Spanish grandees, grasping their stilettos, and frowning vengeance upon the hated Yankees, who stand between them and universal pillage. He sees the flags floating from the ambassadorial palaces,

IN MEXICO.

and groups of elegantly-attired women behind them, peering through their folds upon the spectacle beneath; and in the balconies the gaudy costume of señor and señorita, gazing with varied emotion upon the begrimed and bronzed soldiery before whose resistless valor has sunk every emblem of their independence and sovereignty. He hears the measured tramp of armed columns, the distant roll of artillery wheels, the clash of arms upon the pavement, the sounding hoofs of horses on the street, the inspiriting burst of "Hail to the Chief," as Worth's veteran warriors, drawn up in line of battle upon the Alameda, salute the passing cavalcade of the general-in-chief. On the Grand Plaza, where, in front of the magnificent cathedral, Quitman's division is presenting arms, Grant beholds, in the full uniform of his rank, escorted by a squadron of dragoons, and half hid by the flashing trappings of his staff, the towering form of that chieftain, who, after storming the strongholds of Mexico and annihilating her armies, alights at the steps of her national palace, conscious desert ennobling his lineaments, and the premonitions of an established fame animating his bosom.

The Science of War—General Scott is Grant's Teacher—Theory vs. Practice.

The qualification for the chief of mighty armies is the science of command itself, which teaches where armies shall be stationed, engagements won, and campaigns conducted. You may con the battles and operations of the most celebrated warriors in biographies; you may learn by heart their war maxims, as you may try to master chess without a competitor, or anatomy and surgery without an operating room; but a century of such fancy drill in these arts will never produce a Morphy, a Mott, or a Napoleon.

I have heard General Grant affirm, says Mr. Deming, that, "when he was first intrusted with high military authority, he knew nothing of strategy except what he had learned by critical observation, upon the spot, of the modes and expedients by which the genius of Scott counterbalanced the intrenched positions and the numerical superiority of the Mexicans."

It is a source of profound gratification that such a model campaign, in all respects, was presented for his study and consideration. It has been justly said of it, that it was conducted with fewer strategical mistakes, with less sacrifice of men, with less devastation in proportion to its victories, and with more fidelity to the established laws and usages of war, than that of any invading general upon record.

Entering into and a part of this science of command is that genius—born, not made—by which the great masters of the art magnetize every soldier in the ranks. There is something more in war than what Napoleon's maxim asserts—"the art of being the strongest." The warrior works with instruments that have souls within them. A general may be familiar with all that the books teach of war; he may be expert in every minutia of tactics; he may be accomplished in the theoretical and mechanical parts of strategy; he may have learned all of it which can be taught by study, and also by *experience;* yet if he lack but one thing—this personal ascendency—down to the dust will his banner sink before that antagonist whose sole superiority is the possession of this exalted attribute.

It is this power, which, in the dire extremity, makes one man ten, and a thousand put ten thousand to flight. It was this which Frederick exhibited when his twice ten thousand veterans, inspired by his own genius, vanquished at Rosbach four times ten thousand French and Austrians;

the father and the king exhorting his grenadiers as they passed into the battle-cloud, ".You yourselves know that there have been no watchings, no fatigues, no sufferings, no dangers, which I have not steadily shared with you up to this very hour; and you now see me ready to die with you and for you. All that I ask of you, comrades, is that you return me zeal for zeal and love for love." It was the power of the four consummate warriors of the race—

> " The science of commanding;
> The godlike art of moulding, welding, fettering, banding
> The minds of millions till they move like one."

It can not be reasonably doubted that Scott possessed, to a considerable degree, this inspiring quality of eminent generalship; and it is fortunate, that, for so long a period, Grant dwelt so near the source of inspiration that he may have caught the flame; close to the magnet that he may have imbibed a portion of its mysterious power.

GEN. GRANT'S MARRIAGE.

General Grant's Capture of a "Willing Prisoner"—Her Name Was "Miss Julia"—His Marriage—Social Life in Detroit.

After his war with the gods, Prometheus—so the story goes—was bound to a rock in Caucasus, and an immense vulture sent daily to pounce upon his liver, which grew as fast as it was devoured. His punishment seems to be typical of the tedium which preys upon the mind of the soldier when he passes suddenly from such scenes as Churubusco and Chapultepec to the torpid perceptions and sluggish arterial circulation of a hibernating bear at Fort Desolation.

We never should have heard of Grant, says a friend, after his second imprisonment in one of these dungeons of Despair, but for an incident the most fortunate of his varied career.

He was allowed by his military superiors to select an associate to share his exile from military activity. His choice fell upon one who deserved all his confidence and love. He carried with him to his monotonous duties cheerfulness and consolation in the person of a bride.

He was married in August, 1848, to Miss Julia T. Dent, the daughter of Frederick Dent, a merchant of St. Louis; and the sister of Frederick T. Dent, a classmate at West Point, who has since risen to the rank of brevet brigadier-general, and was the aide of Grant in several engagements, and his assistant secretary of war when he was the head, *ad interim*, of that department.

She has proved herself the kindest and most affectionate of wives; sharing with unabated courage and constancy the trials and disappointments of his early manhood; fully exemplifying the truth of Lord Bacon's aphorism, that "virtue, like precious odors, is most fragrant when incensed or crushed."

Prosperity and renown have since brought to him a cup crowned with blessings; but, among them all, there is no choicer felicity than that the wife of his youth, in the bloom of her years, is permitted to share them.

Fame and position have also entailed their peculiar trials and anxieties; but they are always met with fortitude and composure when cheered and sustained by the companion who has stood beside him in so many emergencies, and in both extremities of fortune.

Washington, at the age of twenty-six, terminated his novitiate, in that French and Indian War which trained him for the Revolution, at Fort du Quesne. At the age of twenty-six, and at the conclusion of Grant's novitiate in the Mexican War which schooled him for the War of the Rebellion, he was stationed at Detroit.

This city, charming in its natural situation, and, by the beauty of its streets and the elegance of its mansions, attractive as a residence, is still more captivating for its society, refined, cultivated, and intellectual, which, descending as it has from the earliest times, is in some measure due to its origin from the most polished nation in the world.

The social parties of Detroit in the winter of 1848-9 delightfully relieved the dull routine of a quartermaster's duty. The new tie which Grant had recently formed, in addition to rendering his own quarters pleasant and inviting, drew him out of himself, from the mess-room and his cigar, to the pleasant and agreeable circles in the city.

Mrs. Grant was herself fond of social pleasures and

amusements, and they soon became far from insupportable to her husband. It is not true, as is generally supposed, that in private life Grant wraps himself up in reticence and reserve. It is only when pressed to divulge prospective military designs, pumped by adroit politicians to indorse party platforms, pestered by those who worship "gab" to play the *role* of stump-orator on every appropriate and inappropriate occasion, that it becomes as inconvenient and impossible for him to speak as it was for Sir Mungo Malagrowther to hear when his withers were wrung by some disagreeable innuendo. In the society of friends, and even strangers worthy of his civility, Grant is found to be well posted on the current themes of conversation.

General McPherson, who was a distinguished division-commander under General Grant, on one occasion said to a friend: "To know and appreciate General Grant fully, one ought to be a member of his military family. Though possessing a remarkable reticence as far as military operations are concerned, he is frank and affable, converses well, and has a peculiarly retentive memory. When not oppressed with the cares of his position, he is very fond of talking and telling anecdotes."

Let it not, therefore, be supposed that Lieut. Grant was not "master of the situation," even in the fashionable circles of Detroit.

IN THE FAR WEST.

General Grant in Oregon—Watching the Indians.

Early in 1852, the Fourth Infantry, in which Grant was still acting quartermaster, was ordered to the Pacific coast. The first station of Grant was at Benicia, where we find him in the fall of 1852. This is a dépôt of ordnance and quartermasters' stores in the Pacific Department; and he is engaged here for a few weeks in making requisitions and shipping supplies, when he is ordered to Fort Vancouver in Oregon.

Grant departs with his regiment to this forlorn spot, isolated from civilization on the east by an intervening wilderness more than two thousand miles in breadth, and from civilization on the west by a coast-range of sombre mountains, which shuts it off even—save by one avenue—from the great highway of nations.

Vancouver is eighty miles from the sea, enveloped in the melancholy shade of primitive forests. When Grant reached it, he found it still retained as one of the central seats of traffic and distribution by the Hudson's Bay Company. During the era of conflicting claims between the United States and Great Britain upon Oregon, it had pushed its pretensions into that territory, wove over it a network of chief and subordinate establishments, and now exercised unlimited control over the nomadic Indians whom the Fourth Infantry had been despatched to quell.

The station of the company, in the center of the clearing, wore all the aspects of a military post. An imposing stockade encloses an area of about seven acres, with mounted bastions at two of its angles; within are the governor's residence, two small buildings for clerks, and a range of dwellings for families; without is another storehouse, under lease to our government; and a few hundred yards farther to the east, rising from a plain upon the very edge of immemorial woods, are the log houses known as the Columbia Barracks; and within an arrow's flight of our flag-staff is a group of hovels, occupied by Indians, servants, and Kanackas.

Four companies of the Fourth are here, with Grant still quartermaster : one company is at Fort Dallas, higher up the Columbia; and the remainder are so distributed as to guard and keep open communication between Oregon and California, with assistant quartermasters for their respective stations.

At this desolate station, Grant vegetated for one year. Cervantes never sent Don Quixote on an adventure more fantastic than the one which the Secretary of War had ordered four companies of an infantry regiment to achieve.

They must guard the trail of emigrants through Oregon; the whole army of the United States could not effectually do it. They must chastise Indian raiders upon the route; winged soldiers, with pinions like a condor to buffet mountain-blasts, might attempt it with some hope of success; but it is utterly beyond the capacity of bipeds moving along the earth.

When a report reaches the garrison that the Indians are at a particular post, you put your finger upon them, and they are not there. Before a company is rallied, the war-party vanishes, and can be captured as easily as the winds which were with them, at the same hour, upon the same occasion.

The sole service of troops at Vancouver is as a moral

CASCADES.

support to the emigrants, and a terror to the wild foe. Even the alarms, which during the first six months temporarily animate the garrison, are soon checked by the adroitness of Lieut.-Col. Bonneville in command, who establishes intimate relations with the servants of the Hudson Bay Company, and, through the instrumentality of its widely-scattered agencies, succeeds in pacifying the tribes.

The second half year opens with the purpose accomplished for which the troops were sent. There is no Indian raider upon the trail, no war-party in the mountains, no war-cloud in the horizon. The emigrant train winds along

the desolate track to Oregon City, without ambuscade or assault. There is no call upon the garrison, except to the drill and to the dress parade: "nothing to do" assails it like a plague.

To Grant's active mind it was inexpressibly irksome. Amusements fail to divert him. Snorting mustangs haunt the plain, bounding beneath the rider as if each muscle were a separate prancer, and the entire horse one "of Ukraine breed." The man born on horseback scorns to bestride them. Gangs of Kanackas, in fantastic attire, mounted on these wild coursers, career and caracole, advance, retreat, wind circle within circle, as they represent mimic battles and hippodromes, before the barrack-door; but they fail to enliven the dull eye of the spectator. An elk of twelve tines, dashing through the underbrush, hardly tempts him to the chase. The salmon—gamiest of fish—leaps the cascades of the Columbia, on its way to the spawning-shoal, in the stupendous defiles of the mountains. The deep pool below fairly whirls and glistens with the arrested silver-backs, which dart at a fly in mid-air, with an eagerness of spring that would have crazed old Izaak Walton, and held him for days absorbed in wild enchantment. Grant throws his line with as much listlessness as if he were bobbing for tadpoles in a tan vat.

THE FARMER.

General Grant a Farmer—He Buys a Farm and Settles Down near St. Louis.

In a period of profound national peace, Capt. Grant discards his epaulets, that he may enjoy domestic life. He resigned his commission as captain in the army July 31, 1854, with the certain knowledge that he must earn a livelihood for himself and family by the labor of his hands and the sweat of his brow: after all, as the Spanish proverb hath it, "the shirt is nearer than the coat."

The choice and the sacrifice equally impress the thoughtful mind, while this new life-discipline produces fruit in the character which is not to be despised. He makes himself a good husband and a good father, and therefore becomes a good citizen. He works, that he may never bend "the pliant hinges of the knee" to power or riches.

Let not proud ambition mock this homely joy bought by useful toil! Labor is twice blessed which duty inspires; and, as old George Herbert says, "The man who sweeps the church makes it and himself to be clean."

The nation is made up of men whose daily life is daily toil; and no one represents its tone, or is fit to govern it, who has not learned by bitter trial that "wealth is best known by want."

Brave souls alone can endure this ordeal; the feeble would die from inanition; the bright would corrode with rust; the impetuous slide into crime; the fanciful fret themselves to death in chasing the chimeras of an impracticable imagination; but the *fort esprit* endures and waits.

U. S. Grant, with his family, removed to Gravois, southwest of St. Louis, where he owned and worked a farm, and from whence he was in the habit of cutting wood, drawing it to Carondelet, and selling it in the market there.

Many of his wood purchasers are now calling to mind that they had a cord of wood delivered in person by the great General Grant.

When he came into the wood market he was usually dressed in an old felt hat, with a blouse coat, and his pants tucked in the tops of his boots. In truth, he bore the appearance of a sturdy, honest woodman. This was his Winter's work.

In the Summer he turned a collector of debts; but for this he was not qualified. He had a noble and truthful soul; so when he was told that the debtor had no money, he believed him, and would not trouble the debtor again.

How many of the illustrious of the earth have endured the same discipline! how many have failed to be illustrious because they have shrunk from bearing this cross!

At the age of thirty-six, Grant was a working husbandman on a Missouri farm.

At the age of thirty-six, Cromwell was a farmer at St. Ives, cultivating his fields, multiplying his flocks and herds.

At the age of thirty-six, Washington was a planter, raising tobacco, and copying his accounts with mercantile neatness and precision.

At thirty-six, Peter the Great was working with his own hands, as a common shipwright, in the dockyards of Amsterdam.

Franklin was not a less deliberate and cautious statesman, because at thirty-six he had been a patient type-setter.

Nor was Sherman a worse counsellor in evil times for having, at the same age, used the awl and the wax-end.

How many have emerged from the humblest positions to the foremost ranks of our citizenship!

Our barefooted plowboys rise to ride the Steed of State, and wield the rod of republican empire.

Our printing-press sends forth its Franklin; our shoemaker's bench, its Roger Sherman; our blacksmith's forge, its General Greene; our rustic inn, its General Putnam; our clockmaker's stool, its John Fitch; our little grocery-shop, its Patrick Henry; the rude habitation of a peasant noble, in the midst of a forest, upon a frontier of civilization, its Daniel Webster; the shanty of a humble Irish emigrant amid the wilds of the Waxhaws, its President Andrew Jackson; a lowly cot upon the 'slashes of the Virginia Hanover,' its Henry Clay; our weaver's loom, its President Fillmore; our machinist's block, its self-taught representative of the industrious masses, N. P. Banks.

"And we may add, that, from the log-cabin of a Kentucky backwoodsman, Abraham Lincoln reaches the chair of President, to reflect more renown than he could inherit from the office, by subsequently ascending that dais in the temple of the world's great men, which only belongs to deliverers of nations and martyrs to liberty, and to the reserved seat upon it, which from the beginning had awaited the coming of the emancipator of a race."

IN ILLINOIS.

Grant as a Citizen of Illinois—His Life in Galena—What He Knows About Leather.

During the year 1859—twenty years ago—Grant became a citizen of Illinois, choosing the City of Galena, in Jo

GOING TO THE STORE.

Daviess County, as his place of abode, where he engaged in the leather trade with his father and a younger brother.

He lived in "a cottage on the hill," with his wife and four children, walking to and fro, from the leather store and back to his house three or four times a day; saying, always with decided emphasis, to almost every casual friend accompanying him, as they picked their broken way, "*If I am ever mayor of Galena I will mend this pavement.*"

His thorough knowledge of the leather business may be inferred from the following stories:

While operating in the vicinity of Vicksburg his professed political friends paid a visit to his headquarters, and after a short time spent in compliments, they touched upon the never-ending subject of politics. One of the party was in the midst of a very flowery speech, using all his rhetorical powers to induce the general, if possible, to view matters in the same light as himself, when he was suddenly stopped by Grant.

"There is no use of talking politics to me. I know nothing about them; and, furthermore, I do not know of any person among my acquaintances who does. But," continued he, " there is one subject with which I am perfectly acquainted; talk of that, and I am your man?"

"What is that, General?" asked the politicians, in great surprise.

" Tanning leather," was the reply.

The subject was immediately changed.

On another occasion an infamous proposal was made by a person to General Grant while he was staying at his headquarters " in the field." The general, irritated, administered a severe kick to the proposer, with the toe of his great cavalry boot ; and, after the fellow had been driven from the tent, one of his staff remarked to a companion, that he did not think the general had hurt the rascal.

" Never fear," was the reply; " that boot never fails under such circumstances, for the leather came from Grant's store, in Galena."

General Smith's Graphic Description of Grant's Galena Life— Laughable Reception by His Regiment.

Sitting round a blazing camp-fire a few evenings since, writes a gentleman in a letter, dated Raleigh, N. C., April 24, 1865, several Illinois officers related their experiences of General Grant in civil life. Here is, as nearly as I can recollect it, what General John E. Smith said on the subject:

"I don't believe any man in Illinois knew Grant better than I did, and I think I had quite as much to do as any other man in bringing him into the war. I lived in Galena at the time. Grant's place of business was near mine. He kept a hardware and saddlery store. I used to drop in to see him very often on my way home, and he and I would generally smoke our pipes together in his office adjoining his store. He was a very poor business man, and never liked to wait on customers. If a customer called in the absence of the clerks, he would tell him to wait a few minutes till one of the clerks returned; and if he couldn't wait, the General would go behind the counter very reluctantly and drag down whatever was wanted; but he hardly ever knew the price of it, and in nine cases out of ten he charged either too much or too little. He would rather talk about the Mexican War than wait upon the best customer in the world.

"When the war broke out, I told him one day that I was going down to Springfield to see Governor Yates, who had sent for me. Grant merely remarked in a quiet way: 'You can say to the Governor that if I can be of any use to him in the organization of these regiments I will be glad to do what I can.'

"I went to Springfield, and made arrangements for Grant to be sent for. He came right down and went to work to organize ten regiments called out as a sort of home guard, for thirty days at first, but afterwards enlisted for three years. When he had done this and was ready to go home, Governor Yates offered him the Coloneley of the Twenty-first Regiment, one of the ten. He accepted it, and immediately went to camp.

THE STATE CAPITOL AT SPRINGFIELD, ILL.

"I went with him, and I shall never forget the scene that occurred when his men first saw him. It was very laughable. Grant was dressed very clumsily, in a suit of citizen's clothes—an old coat worn out at the elbows, and a badly-dinged plug hat. His men, though ragged and barefooted themselves, had formed a high estimate of what a Colonel ought to be; and when Grant walked in among them they began making fun of him. They cried in derision:

"'Look at our Colonel?' 'What a Colonel!' 'Oh, what a Colonel!'—and made all sorts of fun of him.

"A few of them, to 'show off' to the others, got behind his back and began sparring at him; and, while one was doing this, another gave him such a push that made him hit Grant a terrible blow between the shoulders.

"The General soon showed that they must not judge the officer by the uniform, and before he got through, the unruly fellows felt much mortified.

"One of them generously confessed that it was all in fun, and hoped the new Colonel wouldn't get mad about it. Grant went to work immediately, and in a very short time had his men clothed and fixed up in good style."

IN THE REBELLION.

Gov. Yates' Story of How Grant Got into the Army.

On the 13th of April, 1861, Grant heard the news of the fall of Sumter. On the 14th, he began enrolling recruits; on the 19th, he was drilling his volunteers in the streets; on the 23d, he marched with them to Springfield, the capital of Illinois. When he reached this place he wrote a letter to the adjutant-general of the state, rehearsing his antecedents, and offering his skill and experience in arms to the governor, " in whatever situation he may be pleased to place me."

Having received no reply to this communication, he presented himself in person to Gov. Yates, and solicited military employment.

" In presenting himself to me," says Gov. Yates, " Grant made no reference to any merits, but simply said he had been the recipient of a military education at West Point; and, now that the country was assailed, he thought it his duty to offer his services; and that he would esteem it a privilege to be assigned to any position where he could be useful.

" I can not now claim to myself the credit of having discerned in him the promise of great achievements, or the qualities ' which minister to the making of great names,' more than in many others who proposed to enter the military service. His appearance at first sight is not striking. He had no grand airs, no imposing appearance; and I confess, it could not be said he was a form—

Unforgotten.

"'Where every god did seem to set his seal
To give the world assurance of a man.'

"He was plain, very plain; but still something—perhaps his plain, straightforward modesty and earnestness—induced me to assign him a desk in the executive office. In a short time I found him to be an invaluable assistant in my office and in that of the adjutant-general. He was soon after assigned to the command of the six camps of organization and instruction which I had established in the state.

"Early in June, 1861, I telegraphed him at Covington, Ky. (where he had gone on a brief visit to his father), tendering him the colonelcy of the Twenty-first Regiment of Illinois Infantry, which he promptly accepted; and on the 15th of June he assumed the command. The regiment had become much demoralized from lack of discipline, and contention in regard to promotions. On this account Col. Grant, being under marching orders, declined railroad transportation, and, for the sake of discipline, marched them on foot toward the scene of operations in Missouri; and in a short time he had his regiment under perfect control."

The Reported Story that Grant Borrowed Money in Galena to Equip Himself for the War.

Charles A. Washburne, when asked if he had ever heard the story that Elihu Washburne sent General Grant money to equip himself for the war, replied:

"I don't know much about their financial relations. A prominent man in Galena told me this:

"That Grant was called forward to preside at a soldiers' meeting, and he told Elihu, as his Congressman, that he thought it was his duty to go into the army. Elihu gave him a letter to Gov. Yates, recommending him as an ex-officer of the regular army, who had graduated at West Point, and who ought to have a regiment.

"My informant said that Yates put Grant in the Adjutant's office, and set him to copying. After awhile Grant said to the Governor: 'You can get a man to do this work at one dollar a day, and, if this is all you have to give me, I shall go back to Galena.'

"The day following his arrival in Galena I am told that a gentleman saw Grant between daybreak and sunrise walking with Elihu Washburne down to the railroad depot.

"The train which leaves Dunleith, going south, comes through Galena very early in the morning. My brother Elihu was carrying Grant's carpet-bag, and going to the station with him.

"This gentleman says he saw them together, and says that Elihu, as soon as Grant came back from Springfield, told him to return again instantly with a more peremptory letter, and to stay until Yates would give him a regiment.

"If that is true, it is a rather significant thing. Grant might have become a mere Lieutenant or Captain, and not have pressed his way to the front as soon as he did."

Grant's First Movements in the Great Rebellion, and his First Little Speech.

Gen. Grant's first movement in the great rebellion, and it is a singular coincidence, was to pitch his tent in *Mexico*. But this time it was a Missouri village, and belonged to the Western Department of the Army, under the authority of Major General Fremont. He was placed in command of the troops at this point July 31, 1861, but was soon afterwards transferred from Mexico to Ironton, and subsequently to Jefferson City, with no other military care, thus far, than to drill and discipline his own regiment, the

Twenty-first Illinois, and to watch the machinations of the Missouri rebels and partisan gatherings, armed and unarmed, in complicity with treason.

In spite of Grant's limited acquaintance with political leaders, his qualifications for military position had reached the ears of Hon. Elihu B. Washburne, who, for more than twelve years, had represented the Galena district in Congress, but to whom Grant at this time was personally unknown; and upon his recommendation, with the full approval of the colleagues whom he consulted, Grant was commissioned by President Lincoln brigadier-general of volunteers.

His commission was to bear date from May, 1861; and the first intimation or knowledge which Grant received of it was through the daily newspapers.

On the 1st of September, 1861, he assumed command of the *District of Southeast Missouri*, with headquarters at Cairo. *Here his personal responsibility for military operations begins.*

On the 5th of September he heard of Polk's demonstrations within the borders of his district, and forthwith telegraphed the fact to the Kentucky legislature, and to his commanding general for instructions; saying to the latter: "I am getting ready to start for Paducah; will start at six and a half o'clock:" and, later in the afternoon, "I am now ready for Paducah, should not telegram arrive preventing the movement."

He receives no reply. At an early dawn on the morning of the 6th of September, as the rebel general, Tilghman, was drilling recruits in camp at Paducah, he sees the steamer "Mound City" covered with blue coats, the stars and stripes at the gaff, looming out of the fog which had settled on the Ohio. He abdicates immediately, and hurries off with his volunteers by railroad to the south. General Grant marches a detachment ashore, takes possession of the rebel munitions of war, and proclaims, among other things, the following words:

"I am come among you, not as an enemy, but as your fellow-citizen. Not to maltreat you nor annoy you, but to respect and enforce the rights of all loyal citizens. An enemy, in rebellion against our common government, has taken possession of, and planted its guns on the soil of Kentucky, and fired upon you. Columbus and Hickman are in his hands. He is moving upon your city. I am here to defend you against this enemy, to assist the authority and sovereignty of your government. *I have nothing to do with opinions*, and shall deal only with armed rebellion, and its aiders and abettors. You can pursue your usual avocations without fear. The strong arm of the government is here to protect its friends, and punish its enemies. Whenever it is manifest that you are able to defend yourselves, and maintain the authority of the government, and protect the rights of loyal citizens, I shall withdraw the forces under my command."

He leaves a garrison at Paducah, and by twelve o'clock is on his return to Cairo, where he finds permission from Fremont "to move on to Paducah if he feels strong enough!"

General Grant, when in camp at Cairo, presented little, in fact nothing, of the gewgaws and trappings which are generally attached to the attire of a general; and in this respect he showed a marked contrast between himself and some of his sub-lieutenants, whose bright buttons and glittering shoulder-straps were perfectly resplendent. The general, instead, would move about the camp with his attire carelessly thrown on, and left to fall as it pleased. In fact, he seemed to care nothing at all about his personal appearance, and in the place of the usual military hat and ·gold cord, he wore an old battered black hat, generally designated as a "stove-pipe," an article that his subordinates would not have stooped to pick up. In his mouth he carried a black-looking cigar, and he seemed to be perpetually smoking.

General Grant's Private Letter to his Father, Describing the Opening Battle at Belmont.

This was Grant's first battle in the Rebellion. To his father he described it as follows :

"Day before yesterday I left Cairo with about three thousand men, in five steamers, convoyed by two gunboats, and proceeded down the river to within about twelve miles of Columbus. The next morning the boats were dropped down just out of range of the enemy's batteries, and the troops debarked. During this operation our gunboats exercised the rebels by throwing shells into their camps and batteries. When all ready, we proceeded about one mile toward Belmont, opposite Columbus, when I formed the troops into line, and ordered two companies from each regiment to deploy as skirmishers, and push on through the woods and discover the position of the enemy. They had gone but a little way when they were fired upon, and the ball may be said to have fairly opened.

"The whole command, with the exception of a small reserve, was then deployed in like manner and ordered forward. The order was obeyed with great alacrity, the men all showing great courage. I can say with great gratification that every colonel, without a single exception, set an example to their commands that inspired a confidence that will always insure victory when there is the slightest possibility of gaining one. I feel truly proud to command such men.

"From here we fought our way from tree to tree through the woods to Belmont, about two and a half miles, the enemy contesting every foot of ground. Here the enemy had strengthened their position by felling the trees for two or three hundred yards, and sharpening their limbs, making a sort of abatis. Our men charged through, making the victory complete, giving us possession of their camp and garrison equipage, artillery, and everything else.

"We got a great many prisoners. The majority, however, succeeded in getting aboard their steamers and pushing across the river. We burned everything possible and started back, having accomplished all that we went for, and even more. Belmont is entirely covered by the batteries from Columbus, and is worth nothing as a military position—can not be held without Columbus.

"The object of the expedition was to prevent the enemy from sending a force into Missouri to cut off troops I had sent there for a special purpose, and to prevent re-enforcing Price.

"Besides being well fortified at Columbus, their number far exceeded ours, and it would have been folly to have attacked them. We found the Confederates well armed and brave. On our return, stragglers, that had been left in our rear (now front) fired into us, and more recrossed the river and gave us battle for a full mile, and afterward at the boats when we were embarking.

"There was no hasty retreating or running away. Taking into account the object of the expedition, the victory was complete. It has given us confidence in the officers and men of this command, that will enable us to lead them in any future engagement without fear of the result. General McClernand (who, by the way, acted with great coolness and courage throughout, and proved that he is a soldier as well as a statesman) and myself, each had our horses shot under us. Most of the field officers met with the same loss, beside nearly one third of them being themselves killed or wounded. As near as I can ascertain, our loss was about two hundred and fifty killed, wounded, and missing."

General Grant's Own Description of the Battle of Fort Donelson.

In his report of what General Grant's guarded lips always calls "the terrible conflict," the battle of Fort Donelson, he says:

" I left Fort Henry on the 12th instant, with a force of about fifteen thousand men, divided into two divisions, under the command of Generals McClernand and Smith. Six regiments were sent around by water the day before, convoyed by a gunboat (or boats), and with instructions not to pass it.

The troops made the march in good order, the head of the column arriving within two miles of the fort at twelve o'clock M. At this point the enemy's pickets were met and driven in. The fortifications of the enemy were from this point gradually approached and surrounded, with occasional skirmishing on the line.

The following day, owing to the non-arrival of the gunboats and re-enforcements sent by water, no attack was made, but the investment was extended on the flanks of the enemy, and drawn closer to his works, with skirmishing all day.

" On the evening of the 13th, the gunboats and re-enforcements arrived.

" On the 14th, a gallant attack was made by Flag-Officer Foote upon the enemy's river batteries with his fleet. The engagement lasted probably one hour and a half, and bid fair to result favorably, when two unlucky shots disabled two of the armored boats, so that they were carried back by the current. The remaining two were very much disabled, also, having received a number of heavy shots about the pilot-houses and other parts of the vessels.

"After these mishaps, I concluded to make the investment of Fort Donelson as perfect as possible, and partially fortify, and await repairs to the gunboats. This plan was frustrated, however, by the enemy making a most vigorous attack upon our right wing, commanded by Brigadier-General J. A. McClernand, and which consisted of his division and a portion of the force under General L. Wallace.

"The enemy were repelled, after a closely contested battle of several hours, in which our loss was heavy. The officers suffered out of proportion. I have not the means of determining our loss, even approximately, but it can not fall far short of twelve hundred killed, wounded, and missing. Of the latter, I understand, through General Buckner, about two hundred and fifty were taken prisoners. I shall retain here enough of the enemy to exchange for them, as they were immediately shipped off, and not left for recapture.

"About the close of this action the ammunition and cartridge-boxes gave out, which, with the loss of many of the field officers, produced great confusion in the ranks. Seeing that the enemy did not take advantage of it, convinced me that equal confusion, and, consequently, great demoralization, existed with him. Taking advantage of this fact, I ordered a charge upon the left (enemy's right) with the division under General C. F. Smith, which was most brilliantly executed, and gave to our arms full assurance of victory.

"The battle lasted until dark, and gave us possession of part of the intrenchment. An attack was ordered from the other flank after the charge by General Smith was commenced, by the divisions under McClernand and Wallace, which, notwithstanding hours of exposure to a heavy fire in

WAR IN ANCIENT TIMES.

the fore part of the day, was gallantly made, and the enemy further repulsed. At the points thus gained, night having come on, all the troops encamped for the night, feeling that a complete victory would crown their efforts at an early hour in the morning. This morning, at a very early hour, a note was received from General Buckner, under a flag of truce, proposing an armistice."

General Buckner's "note" to Grant on this occasion read as follows:

"SIR: In consideration of all the circumstances governing the present situation of affairs at this station, I propose to the commanding officer of the Federal forces the appointment of commissioners, to agree upon terms of capitulation of the forces and post under my command, and in 'that view suggest an armistice until twelve o'clock to-day."

To which General Grant replied:

"SIR: Yours of this date proposing armistice and appointment of commissioners to settle terms of capitulation, is just received. No terms except unconditional and immediate surrender can be accepted. *I propose to move immediately upon your works.*"

General Buckner surrendered at once his claims to Fort Donelson, with about fifteen thousand prisoners, forty pieces of artillery, and a large amount of stores, horses, mules, and other public property.

After the fall of Fort Donelson, Sherman congratulated Grant warmly on his success, and Grant replied:

" I feel under many obligations to you for the kind terms of your letter, and hope that should an opportunity occur, you will earn for yourself that promotion which you are kind enough to say belongs to me. I care nothing for promotion so long as our arms are successful, and no political appointments are made."

This was the beginning of a friendship destined thereafter never to flag, to stand the test of apparent rivalry and public censure, to remain firm under trials such as few friendships were ever subjected to, to become warmer as often as it was sought to be interrupted, and ·in hours of extraordinary anxiety and responsibility and care, to afford a solace and a support that were never lacking when the need arose.

The Race—Parallel Generals—On a Four-Year Race Grant Comes In Ahead.

The following table exhibits the relative position of General Grant on May 17, 1861, with the others of the same rank, appointed on the same day, and how each of these generals was employed towards the close of the war. It will be noted that U. S. Grant stood No. 17—just half way down the list—at the time he received his brigadier-general's commission. Before the war closed, General Grant was commanding as much territory and as many troops as all the other thirty-three generals combined:

GENERALS.	JANUARY 1, 1864.
Samuel P. Heintzelman	Not in active field service.
Erasmus D. Keyes	do. do.
Andrew Porter	do. do.
Fitz John Porter	Cashiered.
Wm. B. Franklin	Commanding 19th Army Corps.
Wm. T. Sherman	Commanding a Department under General Grant.
Charles P. Stone	Chief of Staff to General Banks.
Don Carlos Buell	Not in active field service.
Thomas W. Sherman	Temporarily invalided.
James Oakes	Not in service.
John Pope	Commanding Department of the Northwest.
George A. McCall	Resigned.
William R. Montgomery	Not in active field service.
Philip Kearney	Dead.

GENERALS.	JANUARY 1, 1864.
Joseph Hooker	Commanding Grand Division under General Grant.
John W. Phelps	Resigned.
ULYSSES S. GRANT	———.
Joseph J. Reynolds	Commanding troops at New Orleans.
Samuel R. Curtis	Not in active field service.
Charles S. Hamilton	do. do.
Darius N. Couch	Commanding Department of the Susquehanna.
Rufus King	Foreign Minister.
J. D. Cox	Commanding Corps under General Grant.
Stephen A. Hurlbut	Commanding Corps under General Grant.
Franz Sigel	Not in active field service.
Robert C. Schenck	In Congress.
B. M. Prentiss	Resigned.
Frederick W. Lander	Dead.
Benj. F. Kelly	Commanding Department of Western Virginia.
John A. McClernand	Not in active field service.
A. S. Williams	Commanding a Division.
I. B. Richardson	Dead.
William Sprague	Declined.
James Cooper	Dead.

General Grant's Words to the "Grand Army."

After General Grant's investment with almost unlimited authority, he utters the following words to the men in the field:

"The major-general commanding this department desires to impress upon all officers the importance of preserving good order and discipline among these troops and the armies of the West, during their advance into Tennessee and the Southern States.

"Let us show to our fellow-citizens of these states, that we come merely to crush out this rebellion, and to restore to them peace and the benefits of the Constitution and the Union, of which they have been deprived by selfish and unprincipled leaders. They have been told that we come to oppress and plunder. By our acts we will undeceive them. We will prove to them that we come to restore, not to violate, the Constitution and the laws. In restoring to them the glorious flag of the Union, we will assure them that they shall enjoy, under its folds, the same protection of life and property as in former days.

"*Soldiers! Let no excesses on your part tarnish the glory of our arms!* The orders heretofore issued from this department in regard to pillaging, marauding, and the destruction of private property, and the stealing and concealment of slaves, must be strictly enforced. It does not belong to the military to decide upon the relation of master and slave. Such questions must be settled by the civil courts.

"No fugitive slave will, therefore, be admitted within our lines or camps, except when especially ordered by the general commanding. *Women and children, merchants, farmers, and all persons not in arms, are to be regarded as non-combatants, and are not to be molested, either in their persons or property.* If, however, they assist and aid the enemy, they become belligerents, and will be treated as such. As they violate the laws of war, they will be made to suffer the penalties of such violation.

"Military stores and public property of the enemy must be surrendered; and any attempt to conceal such property by fraudulent transfer or otherwise will be punished. But no private property will be touched, unless by order of the general commanding.

"Whenever it becomes necessary, forced contributions for supplies and subsistence for our troops will be made. Such levies will be made as light as possible, and be so distributed as to produce no distress among the people. All property so taken must be receipted fully and accepted for as heretofore directed."

The Shiloh Victory, as Described by an Eye-witness.

An eye-witness of this terrific battle, who wrote the first account which appeared in print, describes the thrilling scene, dated April 9, as follows:

One of the greatest and bloodiest battles of modern days has just closed, resulting in the complete rout of the enemy, who attacked us at daybreak Sunday morning.

The battle lasted, without intermission, during the entire day, and was again renewed on Monday morning, and continued undecided until four o'clock in the afternoon, when the enemy commenced their retreat, and are still flying towards Corinth, pursued by a large force of our cavalry.

The slaughter on both sides is immense. We have lost, in killed, wounded, and missing, from eighteen to twenty thousand; that of the enemy is estimated at from thirty-five to forty thousand.

It is impossible, in the present confused state of affairs, to ascertain any of the details; I, therefore, give you the best account possible from observation, having passed through the storm of action during the two days that it raged.

The fight was brought on by a body of three hundred of the Twenty-fifth Missouri Regiment, of General Prentiss' Division, attacking the advance guard of the rebels, which were supposed to be the pickets of the enemy in front of our camps.

The rebels immediately advanced on General Prentiss'

Division on the left wing, pouring volley after volley of musketry, and riddling our camps with grape, canister, and shell. Our forces soon formed into line and returned their fire vigorously. By the time we were prepared to receive them, the rebels had turned their heaviest fire on the left center, Sherman's Division, and drove our men back from their camps; then, bringing up a fresh force, opened fire on our left wing, under General McClernand. This fire was returned with terrible effect and determined spirit by both infantry and artillery, along the whole line, for a distance of over four miles.

General Hurlbut's division was thrown forward to support the center, when a desperate conflict ensued. The rebels were driven back with terrible slaughter, but soon rallied and drove back our men in turn. From about nine o'clock, the time your correspondent arrived on the field, until night closed on the bloody scene, there was no determination of the result of the struggle.

The rebels exhibited remarkably good generalship. At times engaging the left, with apparently their whole strength, they would suddenly open a terrible and destructive fire on the right or centre. Even our heaviest and most destructive fire upon the enemy did not appear to discourage their solid columns. The fire of Major Taylor's Chicago Artillery raked them down in scores, but the smoke would no sooner be dispersed than the breach would again be filled.

The most desperate fighting took place late in the afternoon. The rebels knew that, if they did not succeed in whipping us then, their chances for success would be extremely doubtful, as a portion of Gen. Buell's forces had by this time arrived on the opposite side of the river, and another portion was coming up the river from Savannah. They became aware that we were being re-enforced, as they could see General Buell's troops from the river bank, a short distance above us on the left, to which point they had forced their way.

At five o'clock the rebels had forced our left wing back so as to occupy fully two thirds of our camp, and were fighting their way forward with a desperate degree of confidence in their efforts to drive us into the river, and at the same time heavily engaged our right.

Up to this time we had received no re-enforcements, General Lewis Wallace failing to come to our support until the day was over. Being without other transports than those used for quartermaster's and commissary stores, which were too heavily laden to ferry any considerable number of General Buell's forces across the river, and the boats that were here having been sent to bring up the troops from Savannah, we could not even get those men to us who were so near, and anxiously waiting to take part in the struggle. We were, therefore, contesting against fearful odds, our force not exceeding thirty-eight thousand men, while that of the enemy was upwards of sixty thousand.

Our condition at this moment was extremely critical. Large numbers of men panic struck, others worn out by hard fighting, with the average percentage of skulkers, had straggled towards the river, and could not be rallied.

General Grant and staff, who had been recklessly riding along the lines during the entire day, amid the unceasing storm of bullets, grape, and shell, now rode from right to left, inciting the men to stand firm until our re-enforcements could cross the river.

Colonel Webster, Chief of Staff, immediately got into position the heaviest pieces of artillery, pointing on the enemy's right, while a large number of the batteries were planted along the entire line, from the river bank northwest to our extreme right, some two and a half miles distant. About an hour before dusk a general cannonading was opened upon the enemy, from along our whole line, with a perpetual crack of musketry. Such a roar of artillery was never heard on this continent. For a short time the rebels replied with vigor and effect, but their return shots grew less frequent and destructive, while ours grew more rapid and more terrible.

The gunboats Lexington and Tyler, which lay a short distance off, kept raining shell on the rebel hordes. This last effort was too much for the enemy, and ere dusk had set in the firing had nearly ceased, when, night coming on, all the combatants rested from their awful work of blood and carnage.

Our men rested on their arms in the position they had at the close of the night, until the forces under Major-General Lewis Wallace arrived and took position on the right, and General Buell's forces from the opposite side and Savannah, were being conveyed to the battle-ground. The entire right of General Nelson's division was ordered to form on the right, and the forces under General Crittenden were ordered to his support early in the morning.

General Buell, having himself arrived on Sunday evening, on the morning of Monday, April 7, the ball was opened at daylight, simultaneously by General Nelson's division on the left, and Major-General Wallace's division on the right. General Nelson's force opened up a most galling fire on the rebels, and advanced rapidly as they fell back. The fire soon became general along the whole line, and began to tell with terrible effect on the enemy. Generals McClernand, Sherman, and Hurlbut's men, though terribly jaded from the previous day's fighting, still maintained their honors won at Donelson; but the resistance of the rebels at all points of the attack was terrible, and worthy of a better cause.

But they were not enough for our undaunted bravery and the dreadful desolation produced by our artillery, which was sweeping them away like chaff before the wind. But knowing that a defeat here would be the death-blow to their hopes, and that their all depended on this great struggle, their generals still urged them on in the face of destruction, hoping by flanking us on the right to turn the tide of battle. Their success was again for a time cheering, as they began to gain ground on us, appearing to have been re-enforced; but our left, under General Nelson, was driving them, and with wonderful rapidity, and by eleven o'clock General Buell's forces had succeeded in flanking them and capturing their batteries of artillery.

They, however, again rallied on the left, and recrossed, and the right forced themselves forward in another desperate effort. But re-enforcements from General Wood and General Thomas were coming in, regiment after regiment, which were sent to General Buell, who had again commenced to drive the enemy.

About three o'clock in the afternoon, General Grant rode to the left where the fresh regiments had been ordered, and, finding the rebels wavering, sent a portion of his body guard to the head of each of five regiments, and then ordered a charge across the field, himself leading; and as he brandished his sword and waved them on to the crowning victory, the cannon balls were falling like hail around him.

The men followed with a shout that sounded above the roar and din of the artillery, and the rebels fled in dismay as from a destroying avalanche, and never made another stand.

General Buell followed the retreating rebels, driving them in splendid style, and by half-past five o'clock the whole rebel army was in full retreat to Corinth, with our cavalry in hot pursuit, with what further result is not known, not having returned up to this hour.

We have taken a large amount of their artillery and also a number of prisoners. We lost a number of our forces prisoners yesterday, among whom is General Prentiss. The number of our force taken has not yet been ascertained. It is reported at several hundred. General Prentiss was also reported as being wounded. Among the killed on the rebel side, was their General-in-Chief, Albert Sydney Johnston, who was struck by a cannon ball on the afternoon of Sunday. Of this there is no doubt, and it is further reported that General Beauregard was wounded.

This afternoon, Generals Bragg, Breckinridge and Jackson were commanding portions of the rebel forces.

There has never been a parallel to the gallantry and bearing of our officers, from the commanding general to the lowest officer.

General Grant and staff were in the field, riding along the lines in the thickest of the enemy's fire during the entire two days of the battle, and all slept on the ground Sunday night, during a heavy rain. On several occasions General Grant got within range of the enemy's guns and was discovered and fired upon.

Lieutenant-Colonel McPherson had his horse shot from under him when alongside of General Grant.

Captain Carson was between General Grant and your correspondent when a cannon ball took off his head and killed and wounded several others.

General Sherman had two horses killed under him, and General McClernand shared like dangers; also General Hurlbut, each of whom received bullet holes through their clothes.

The following compliment from Washington was sent at the close of the battle:

"The thanks of the Department are hereby given to Major-Generals Grant and Buell and their forces, for the glorious repulse of Beauregard at Pittsburg, in Tennessee."

The Siege of Corinth—An Eloquent Description by a Participant.

A graphic description of what constitutes a battle and of what occurred at Corinth is given by one who participated, as follows:

"First, the enemy must be driven back. Regiments and artillery are placed in position, and generally the cavalry is in advance, but when the opposing forces are in close proximity the infantry does the work. The whole front is covered by a cloud of skirmishers, and then reserves are formed, and then, in connection with the main line, they advance. For a moment all is still as the grave to those in the background; as the line moves on, the eye is strained in vain to follow the skirmishers as they creep silently forward; then, from some point of line, a single rifle rings through the forest, sharp and clear, and, as if in echo, another answers it. In a moment more the whole line resounds with the din of arms. Here the fire is slow and steady, there it rattles with fearful rapidity, and this mingled with the great roar of the reserves as the skirmishers chance at any point to be driven in; and if, by reason of superior force, these reserves fall back to the main force, then every nook and corner seems full of sound. The batteries open their terrible voices, and their shells sing horribly while winging their flight, and their dull explosion speaks plainly of death; their canister and grape go crashing through the trees, rifles ring, the muskets roar, and the din is terrific. Then the slackening of the fire denotes the withdrawing of the one party, and the more distant picket-firing, that the work was accomplished. The silence becomes almost painful after such a scene as this, and no one can conceive of the effect who has not experienced it; it can not be described. The occasional firing of pickets, which shows that the new lines are established, actually occasions a sense of relief. The movements of the mind under such circumstances are sudden and strong. It awaits with intense anxiety the opening of the contest, it rises with the din of battle, it sinks with the lull which follows it, and finds itself in fit condition to sympathize most deeply with the torn and bleeding ones which are fast being borne to the rear.

"When the ground is clear, then the time for working parties has arrived, and, as this is the description of a real scene, let me premise that the works were to reach through the center of a large open farm of at least three hundred acres, surrounded by woods, one side of it being occupied by rebel pickets. These had been driven back as I have described.

"The line of the works was selected, and at the word of command three thousand men, with axes, spades, and picks, stepped out into the open field from their cover in the woods; in almost as short a time as it takes to tell it, the fence-rails which surrounded and divided three hundred acres into convenient farm lots were on the shoulders of the men, and on the way to the intended line of works. In a few moments more a long line of crib-work stretches over the slope of the hill, as if another anaconda fold had been twisted around the rebels. Then, as for a time, the ditches deepen, the cribs fill up, the dirt is packed on the other side, the bushes and all points of concealment are cleared from the front, and the center divisions of our army had taken a long stride towards the rebel works. The siege-guns are brought up and placed in commanding positions. A log house furnishes the hewn and seasoned timber for the platforms, and the plantation of a Southern lord has been thus speedily transferred into one of Uncle Sam's strongholds, where the stars and stripes float proudly. Thus had the whole army (under the immediate charge of General Grant, the commander in the field) worked itself up into the very teeth of the rebel works, and rested there on Thursday night, the twenty-eighth, expecting a general engagement at any moment.

"Soon after daylight, on Friday morning, the army was startled by rapid and long-continued explosions, similar to musketry, but much louder. The conviction flashed across my mind that the rebels were blowing up their loose ammunition and leaving. The dense smoke arising in the direction of Corinth strengthened this belief, and soon the whole army was advancing on a grand reconnoissance. The distance through the woods was short, and in a few minutes shouts arose from the rebel lines, which told that our army was in the enemy's trenches. Regiment after regiment pressed on, and, passing through extensive camps just vacated, soon reached Corinth and found half of it in flames. Beauregard and Bragg had left the afternoon before, and the rear guard had passed out of the town before daylight, leaving enough stragglers to commit many acts of vandalism, at the expense of private property. They burned churches and other public buildings, private goods, stores and other dwellings, and choked up half the wells in town. In the camps immediately around the town there were few evidences of hasty retreat, but on the right flank, where Price and Van Dorn were encamped, the destruction of baggage and stores was very great, showing precipitate flight. Portions of our army were immediately put in pursuit.

"It seems that it was the slow and careful approach of General Halleck which caused the retreat. They would doubtless have remained had we attacked their positions without first securing our rear, but they could not stand a siege. Their position was a most commanding one and well protected."

A Confederate's Graphic Story of the Battle of Iuka.

A confederate soldier who took part in the struggle at Iuka, gives the following description in a private letter to a friend:

"We held peaceable possession of Iuka for one day, and on the next were alarmed by the booming of cannon, and were called out to spend the evening in battle array in the woods. On the evening of the 19th, when we supposed we were going back to camp, to rest awhile, the sharp crack of musketry on the right of our former lines, told us that the enemy was much nearer than we imagined. In fact, they almost penetrated the town itself. How on earth, with the woods full of our cavalry, they could have approached so near our lines, is a mystery. They had planted a battery sufficiently near to shell General Price's head-quarters, and were cracking away at the Third Brigade when the Fourth came up at double-quick, and then, for two hours and fifteen minutes, was kept up the most terrific fire of musketry that ever dinned my ears. There was one continuous roar of small arms, while grape and canister howled in fearful concert above our heads and through our ranks. General Little was shot dead early in the action. * * * It was a terrible struggle, and we lost heavily. All night could be heard the groans of the wounded and dying, forming a sequel of horror and agony to the deadly struggle, over which night had kindly thrown its mantle. Saddest of all, our dead were left unburied, and many of the wounded on the battle-field to be taken in charge by the enemy.

"Finding that the enemy were being re-enforced from the north, and as our strength would not justify us in trying another battle, a retreat was ordered, and we left the town during the night. The enemy pressed our rear the next day, and were only kept off by grape and canister.

"It grieves me to state that acts of vandalism, disgraceful to any army, were, however, perpetrated along the line of retreat, and makes me blush to own such men as my countrymen. Corn-fields were laid waste, potato patches robbed, barn-yards and smoke-houses despoiled, hogs killed, and all kinds of outrages perpetrated in broad daylight and in full view of the officers. The advance and retreat were alike disgraceful, and I have no doubt that women and children along the route will cry for the bread which has been rudely taken from them by those who should have protected and defended them."

General Grant's Address.

After, the victory, of what General Grant calls the "Memorable Field of Iuka," he addressed—with his pen —his fellow soldiers in the following eloquent words:

"The general commanding takes great pleasure in congratulating two wings of the army, commanded respectively by Major-General Ord and Major-General Rosecrans, upon the energy, alacrity, and bravery displayed by them on the 19th and 20th inst., in their movement against the enemy at Iuka. Although the enemy was in numbers reputed far greater than their own, nothing was evinced by the troops but a burning desire to meet him, whatever his numbers, and however strong his position.

"With such a disposition as was manifested by the troops on this occasion, their commanders need never fear defeat against anything but overwhelming numbers.

"While it was the fortune of the command of General Rosecrans, on the evening of the 19th inst., to engage the enemy in a most spirited fight for more than two hours, driving him, with great loss, from his position, and winning for themselves fresh laurels, the command of General Ord is entitled to equal credit for their efforts in trying to reach the enemy, and in diverting his attention.

"And while congratulating the noble living, it is meet to offer our condolence to the friends of the heroic dead, who offered their lives a sacrifice in defense of constitutional liberty, and in their fall rendered memorable the field of Iuka."

Explosion of the Great Vicksburg Mine and Capture of That City.

As might be supposed, the explosion was designated as the signal for a general simultaneous co-operation all along the lines from right to left.

Every thing was finished. The vitalizing spark had quickened the hitherto passive agent, and the now harmless flashes went hurrying to the center. The troops had been withdrawn. The forlorn hope stood out in plain view, boldly awaiting the uncertainties of the precarious office. A chilling sensation ran through the frame as an observer looked down upon this devoted band about to hurl itself into the breach—perchance into the jaws of death.

Thousands of men in arms flashed on every hill. Every one was speechless Even men of tried valor—veterans insensible to the shouts of contending battalions, or nerved

Storm.

to the shrieks of comrades suffering under the torture of painful agonies—stood motionless as they directed their eyes upon the spot where soon the terror of a buried agency would discover itself in wild concussions and contortions, carrying annihilation to all within the scope of its tremendous power.

It was the seeming torpor which precedes the antagonism of powerful bodies. Five minutes had elapsed. It seemed like an existence. Five minutes more, and yet no signs of the expected exhibition. An indescribable sensation of impatience, blended with a still active anticipation, ran through the assembled spectators.

A small pall of smoke now discovered itself; every one thought the crisis had come, and almost saw the terrific scene which the mind had depicted. But not yet. Every eye now centered upon the smoke, momentarily growing greater and greater. Thus another five minutes wore away, and curiosity was not satisfied. Another few minutes, then the *terrific earth-shaking explosion occurred.* So terrible a spectacle is seldom witnessed. Dust, dirt, smoke, gabions, stockades, timber, gun-carriages, logs—in fact, every thing connected with the fort—rose hundreds of feet into the air, as if vomited forth from a volcano. Some who were close spectators even say that they saw the bodies of the poor wretches who a moment before had lined the ramparts of the work.

One entire face of the fort was disembodied and scattered in pàrticles all over the surrounding surface. The right and left faces were also much damaged; but fortunately enough of them remained to afford an excellent protection on our flanks.

No sooner had the explosion taken place than the two detachments acting as the forlorn hope ran into the fort and sap, as already mentioned. A brisk musketry fire at once commenced between the two parties, with about equal effect upon either side. No sooner had these detachments become well engaged than the rest of Leggett's Brigade joined them and entered into the struggle.

The regiments relieving each other at intervals, the contest now grew severe; both sides, determined upon holding their own, were doing their best. Volley after volley was fired, though with less carnage than would be supposed. The Forty-fifth Illinois charged immediately up to the crest of the parapet, and here suffered its heaviest, losing many officers in the assault.

After a severe contest of half an hour, with varying results, the flag of the Forty-fifth appeared upon the summit of the work. The position was gained. Cheer after cheer broke through the confusion and uproar of the contest, assuring the troops everywhere along the line that the Forty-fifth was still itself. The colonel was now left alone in command of the regiment, and he was himself badly bruised by a flying splinter. The regiment had also suffered severely in the line, and the troops were worn out by excessive heat and hard fighting.

During the hottest of the action General Leggett was in the fort in the midst of his troops, sharing their dangers and partaking of their glory. While here a shell from one of the enemy's guns exploded in a timber lying on the parapet, distributing splinters in all directions, one of which struck the general on the breast, knocking him over. Though somewhat bruised and stunned, he soon recovered himself, and taking a chair, sat in one of the trenches near the fort, where he could be seen by his men.

The explosion of the mine was the signal for the opening of the artillery of the entire line. The left division of General McPherson's Seventeenth, or center, Corps opened first, and discharges were repeated along the left through General Ord's Thirteenth Corps, and Herron's extreme "left division," until the sound struck the ear like the mutterings of distant thunder.

General Sherman, on the right, also opened his artillery about the same time and occupied the enemy's attention along his front. Every shell struck the parapet, and, bounding over, exploded in the midst of the enemy's forces beyond. The scene at this time was one of the utmost sublimity.

The roar of artillery, rattle of small arms, the cheers of the men, flashes of light, wreaths of pale blue smoke over different parts of the field, the bursting of shells, the fierce whistle of solid shot, the deep boom of the mortars, the broadsides of the ships of war, and, added to all this, the vigorous replies of the enemy, set up a din which beggars all description. The peculiar configuration of the field afforded an opportunity to witness almost every battery and every rifle-pit within seeing distance, and it is due to all the troops to say that every one did his duty.

After the possession of the fort was no longer in doubt, the pioneer corps mounted the work with their shovels and set to throwing up earth vigorously in order to secure space for artillery. A most fortunate peculiarity in the explosion was the manner in which the earth was thrown out. The appearance of the place was that of a funnel, with heavy sides running up to the very crest of the parapet, affording admirable protection not only for our troops and pioneers, but turned out a ready made fortification in the rough, which, with a slight application of the shovel and pick, was ready to receive the guns to be used at this point.

From a lookout on the summit of an eminence near the rebel works the movements of the enemy could be plainly watched. An individual in the tower, just prior to the explosion of the mine, saw two rebel regiments marching out to the fort. Of a sudden—perhaps upon seeing the smoke of the fuse—the troops turned about and ran toward the town in perfect panic. They were not seen again during the fight; but other regiments were brought up to supply their place.

Vicksburg's Surrender—An Interesting Interview Between General Grant and the Confederate General, Pemberton.

The following account of the interview between Generals Grant and Pemberton, before Vicksburg, is given by one who had followed the army during the whole campaign:

"At three o'clock precisely, one gun, the prearranged signal, was fired, and immediately replied to by the enemy. General Pemberton then made his appearance on the works in McPherson's front, under a white flag, considerably on the left of what is known as Fort Hill. General Grant rode through our trenches until he came to an outlet, leading to a small green space, which had not been trod by either army. Here he dismounted, and advanced to meet General Pemberton, with whom he shook hands, and greeted familiarly.

"It was beneath the outspreading branches of a gigantic oak that the conference of the generals took place. Here presented the only space which had not been used for some purpose or other by the contending armies. The ground was covered with a fresh, luxuriant verdure; here and there a shrub or clump of bushes could be seen standing out from the green growth on the surface, while several oaks filled up the scene, and gave it character. Some of the trees in their tops exhibited the effects of flying projectiles, by the loss of limbs or torn foliage, and in their trunks the indentations of smaller missiles plainly marked the occurrences to which they had been silent witnesses.

"The party made up to take part in the conference was composed as follows:

"United States officers: Major-General U. S. Grant, Major-General James B. McPherson, Brigadier-General A. J. Smith. Confederate officers: Lieutenant-General John C. Pemberton, Major-General Bowen, Colonel Montgomery, A. A. G. to General Pemberton.

"When Generals Grant and Pemberton met they shook hands, Colonel Montgomery introducing the party. A short silence ensued, at the expiration of which General Pemberton remarked:

"'General Grant, I meet you in order to arrange terms for the capitulation of the City of Vicksburg and its garrison. What terms do you demand?'

"'Unconditional surrender,' replied General Grant.

"'Unconditional surrender?' said Pemberton. 'Never, so long as I have a man left me! I will fight rather.'

"'Then, sir, you can continue the defense,' coolly said General Grant. 'My army has never been in a better condition for the prosecution of the siege.'

"During the passing of these few preliminaries, General Pemberton was greatly agitated, quaking from head to foot, while General Grant experienced all his natural self-possession, and evinced not the least sign of embarrassment.

"After a short conversation standing, by a kind of mutual tendency the two generals wandered off from the rest of the party and seated themselves on the grass, in a cluster of bushes, where alone they talked over the important events then pending. General Grant could be seen, even at that distance, talking coolly, occasionally giving a few puffs at his favorite companion—his black cigar. General

McPherson, General A. J. Smith, General Bowen, and Colonel Montgomery, imitating the example of the commanding generals, seated themselves at some distance off, while the respective staffs of the generals formed another and larger group in the rear.

"After a lengthy conversation the generals separated. General Pemberton did not come to any conclusion on the matter, but stated his intention to submit the matter to a council of general officers of his command; and, in the event of their assent, the surrender of the city should be made in the morning.

"Until morning was given him to consider, to determine upon the matter and send in his final reply. The generals now rode to their respective quarters.

"The final reply of General Pemberton, as the world knows, came July 4 (1863), and Vicksburg was surrendered."

President Lincoln's Congratulations to General Grant, and Lincoln's Little Joke.

When the news of this glorious victory at Vicksburg officially reached the President, he wrote an autograph letter to General Grant, as follows:

"MY DEAR GENERAL:—I do not remember that you and I ever met personally. I write this now as a grateful acknowledgment for *the almost inestimable service you have done the country.* I wish to say a word furtner. When you first reached the vicinity of Vicksburg, I thought you should do what you finally did—march the troops across the neck, run the batteries with the transports, and thus go below; and I never had any faith, except a general hope that you knew better than I, that the Yazoo Pass expedition and the like could succeed. When you got below and took Port Gibson, Grand Gulf, and vicinity, I thought you should go down the river and join General Banks; and when you turned northward east of the Big Black, I feared it was a mistake. I now wish to make a personal acknowledgment *that you were right and I was wrong.*"

Several gentlemen were near the President at the time he received the news of Grant's success, some of whom had been complaining of the rumors of his habit of using intoxicating drinks to excess.

"So I understand Grant drinks whisky to excess?" interrogatively remarked the President.

"Yes," was the reply.

"What whisky does he drink?" inquired Mr. Lincoln.

"What whisky?" doubtfully queried his hearers.

"Yes. Is it Bourbon or Monongahela?"

"Why do you ask, Mr. President?"

"Because, if it makes him win victories like this at Vicksburg, I will send a demijohn of the same kind to every general in the army."

His visitors saw the point, although at their own cost.

General Grant's Private Letter to Sherman on the Lieutenant-Generalship.

"DEAR SHERMAN:—The Bill reviving the grade of lieutenant-general in the army has become a law, and my name has been sent to the Senate for the place. I now receive orders to report to Washington immediately, *in person*, which indicates a confirmation, or a likelihood of confirmation. I start in the morning to comply with the order.

"Whilst I have been eminently successful in this war, in at least gaining the confidence of the public, no one feels more than I, how much of this success is due to the energy, skill, and the harmonious putting forth of that energy and skill, of those whom it has been my good fortune to have occupying subordinate positions under me.

"There are many officers to whom these remarks are applicable to a greater or less degree, proportionate to their ability as soldiers; but what I want is to express my thanks to you and McPherson, as the men to whom, above all others, I feel indebted for whatever I have had of success.

"How far your advice and assistance have been of help to me, you know. How far your execution of whatever has been given to you to do, entitles you to the reward I am receiving, you can not know as well as I.

"I feel all the gratitude this letter would express, giving it the most flattering construction.

"The word *you* I use in the plural, intending it for McPherson, also. I should write to him, and will some day, but starting in the morning, I do not know that I will find time just now."

General Grant and President Lincoln in Washington.

On the 8th of March General Grant arrived at Washington, where he had never spent more than one day before. President Lincoln had never seen his face, and the Secretary of War had met him, for the first time, at Louisville, in the October preceding.

At one o'clock, on the 9th of March, Grant was formally received by the President, in the cabinet chamber. There were present all the members of his cabinet, Major-General Halleck, general-in-chief, two members of General Grant's staff, the President's secretary, a single member of Congress, and Grant's eldest son, who had been with him at Jackson, and Vicksburg, and at Champion's Hill.

After Grant had been presented to the members of the cabinet, Mr. Lincoln read the following words: "General Grant, the nation's appreciation of what you have done, and its reliance upon you for what remains to be done in the existing great struggle, are now presented, with this commission constituting you lieutenant-general in the Army of the United States. With this high honor, devolves upon you, also, a corresponding responsibility. As the country herein trusts you, so, under God, it will sustain you. I scarcely need to add, that, with what I here speak for the nation, goes my own hearty personal concurrence."

Grant read, from a paper, this reply: "Mr. President, I accept the commission, with gratitude, for the high honor conferred. With the aid of the noble armies that have fought in so many fields, for our common country, it will be my earnest endeavor not to disappoint your expectations. I feel the full weight of the responsibilities now devolving on me; and I know that if they are met, it will be due to those armies, and above all, to the favor of that Providence which leads both nations and men."

General Lee's Surrender to General Grant—The Decisive Letters Which Ended the Rebellion—Grant's Own Account of His Meeting Lee.

"Feeling," says General Grant, "that Lee's chance of escape was utterly hopeless, I addressed him the following communication from Farmville:"

APRIL 7, 1865.

GENERAL:—The result of the last week must convince you of the hopelessness of further resistance, on the part of the Army of Northern

Virginia, in this struggle. I feel that it is so, and regard it as my duty to shift from myself the responsibility of any further effusion of blood by asking of you the surrender of that portion of the Confederate States army known as the Army of Northern Virginia.

U. S. GRANT, *Lieutenant-General.*

Early on Saturday morning, before leaving Farmville, Grant received the following reply:

APRIL 7, 1865.

GENERAL:—I have received your note of this date. Though not entertaining the opinion you express on the hopelessness of further resistance on the part of the Army of Northern Virginia, I reciprocate your desire to avoid useless effusion of blood, and, therefore, before considering your proposition, ask the terms you will offer on condition of its surrender.

R. E. LEE, *General.*

In answer to this communication, Grant wrote General Lee as follows:

APRIL 8, 1865.

GENERAL:—Your note of last evening, in reply to mine of same date, asking the condition on which I will accept the surrender of the Army of Northern Virginia, is just received. In reply, I would say, that *peace* being my great desire, there is but one condition I would insist upon; namely, that the men and officers surrendered shall be disqualified for taking up arms again against the Government of the United States, until properly exchanged. I will meet you, or will designate officers to meet any officers you may name for the same purpose, at any point agreeable to you, for the purpose of arranging definitely the terms upon which the surrender of the Army of Northern Virginia will be received.

U. S. GRANT, *Lieutenant-General.*

After the reception of this letter, General Lee's prospects had improved, when he indicted the following epistle:

APRIL 8, 1865.

GENERAL:—I received at a late hour your note of to-day. In mine of yesterday I did not intend to propose the surrender of the Army of Northern Virginia, but to ask the terms of your proposition. To be frank, I do not think the emergency has arisen to call for the surrender of this army; but, as the restoration of peace should be the sole object of all, I desired to know whether your proposals would lead to that end. I can not, therefore, meet you with a view to surrender the Army of Northern Virginia; but, as far as your proposal may affect the Confederate States forces under my command, and tend to the restoration of peace, I should be pleased to meet you at ten A. M., to-morrow, on the old stage-road to Richmond, between the picket lines of the two armies.

R. E. LEE, General.

To this General Grant replied:

APRIL 9, 1865.

GENERAL:—Your note of yesterday is received. I have no authority to treat on the subject of peace. The meeting proposed for ten A. M., to-day, could lead to no good. I will state, however, General, that I am equally anxious for peace with yourself; and the whole North entertains the same feeling. The terms upon which peace can be had are well understood. By the South laying down their arms, they will hasten that most desirable event, save thousands of human lives, and hundreds of millions of property not yet destroyed. Seriously hoping that all our difficulties may be settled without the loss of another life, I subscribe myself, etc.

U. S. GRANT, Lieutenant-General.

After transmitting this letter, General Grant immediately started to join Sheridan's column south of Appomattox Court house; for he had received a dispatch from that officer inciting him to press on with all speed, that there was now no means of escape, for the enemy had finally reached the "last ditch." While spurring on to assume direction of affairs in front of Lee, Grant received this letter from the Confederate commander, which had been delivered to Custer by the flag of truce:

APRIL 9, 1865.

GENERAL:—I received your note of this morning on the picket line, whither I had come to meet you, and ascertain definitely what terms were embraced in your proposal of yesterday with reference to the surrender of this army. I now ask an interview, in accordance with the offer contained in your letter of yesterday for that purpose.

R. E. LEE, General.

Grant forthwith penned on his saddle, upon a leaf torn from his tablets, the following reply:

APRIL 9, 1865.
Gen. R. E. LEE, Commanding C. S. A.:
Your note of this date is but this moment, 11:59 A. M., received. In consequence of my having passed from the Richmond and Lynchburg Road to the Farmville and Lynchburg Road, I am, at this writing, about four miles west of Walter's Church, and will push forward to the front for the purpose of meeting you. Notice sent to me on this road where you wish the interview to take place will meet me.
Very respectfully, your obedient servant,
U. S. GRANT, *Lieutenant-General*.

These notes produced the memorable interview between the two commanders at the dwelling of Mr. Wilmer McLean, near Appomattox Court-house.

In describing this meeting General Grant says:

"I felt some embarrassment in the prospect of meeting General Lee. I had not seen him since he was General Scott's chief-of-staff in Mexico; and, in addition to the respect I entertained for him, the duty which I had to perform was a disagreeable one, and I wished to get through it as soon as possible.

"When I reached Appomattox Court-house, I had ridden that morning thirty-seven miles. I was in my campaign clothes, covered with dust and mud; I had no sword; I was not even well mounted, for I rode (turning to General Ingals, who was present) one of Ingals' horses.

"I found General Lee in a fresh suit of Confederate gray, with all the insignia of his rank, and at his side the splendid dress-sword which had been given to him by the State of Virginia. We shook hands. He was exceedingly courteous in his address, and we seated ourselves at a deal table in Mr. McLean's front room.

"We talked of two of the conditions of surrender, which had been left open by our previous correspondence, one of which related to the ceremonies which were to be observed on the occasion; and when I disclaimed any desire to have any parade, but said I should be contented with the delivery of arms to my officers, and with the proper signature and authentication of paroles, he seemed to be greatly pleased.

"When I yielded the other point, that the officers should retain their side arms and private baggage and horses, his emotions of satisfaction were plainly visible. We soon reduced the terms to writing.

"We parted with the same courtesies with which we had met. It seemed to me that General Lee evinced a feeling of satisfaction and relief when the business was finished. I immediately mounted Ingals' horse, returned to General Sheridan's headquarters, and did not again present myself to the Confederate Commander."

The documents signed at Mr. McLean's house were as follows:

APPOMATTOX COURT HOUSE, VA., April 9, 1865.

GENERAL:—In accordance with the substance of my letter to you of the 8th instant, I propose to receive the surrender of the Army of Northern Virginia on the following terms, to wit: rolls of all the officers and men to be made in duplicate, one copy to be given to an officer to be designated by me, the other to be retained by such officer or officers as you may designate. The officers to give their individual paroles not to take up arms against the Government of the United States until properly exchanged, and each company or regimental commander sign a like parole for the men of their commands. The arms, artillery, and public property to be parked and stacked, and turned over to the officers appointed by me to receive them. This will not embrace the side arms of the officers nor their private horses or baggage. This done, each officer and man will be allowed to return to his home, not to be disturbed by the United States authority so long as they observe their paroles, and the laws in force where they may reside.

U. S. GRANT, *Lieutenant-General.*

IN THE REBELLION. 137

HEADQUARTERS ARMY OF NORTHERN VIRGINIA, April 9, 1865.
GENERAL:—I received your letter of this date, containing the terms of the surrender of the Army of Northern Virginia as proposed by you. As they are substantially the same as those expressed in your letter of the 8th instant, they are accepted. I will proceed to designate the proper officers to carry the stipulations into effect.
R. E. LEE, *General.*

Thus was the act engrossed which disbanded and disarmed the Army of Northern Virginia, relegated its veteran officers and soldiers to the ranks of peaceful citizens, and virtually closed the rebellion.

Lieutenant-General Grant's Farewell Address to the Soldiers.

The Union armies under command of Lieutenant-General Grant numbered 1,000,516 soldiers. Their commander might well be proud of the great services which with him they had performed for the country. The following are the great General's parting words:

"SOLDIERS OF THE ARMIES OF THE UNITED STATES:—By your patriotic devotion to your country in the hour of danger and alarm, your magnificent fighting, bravery and endurance, you have maintained the supremacy of the Union and the Constitution, overthrown all armed opposition to the enforcement of the laws and the proclamations forever abolishing slavery—the cause and pretext of the Rebellion—and opened the way to the rightful authorities to restore order, and inaugurate peace on a permanent and enduring basis on every foot of American soil. Your marches, sieges and battles, in distance, duration, resolution and brilliancy of results, dim the lustre of the world's past military achievements, and will be the patriot's precedent in the defense of liberty and right in all time to come. In obedience to your country's call, you left your homes and families, and volunteered in her defense. Victory has crowned your valor and secured the purpose of your patriotic hearts; and with the gratitude of your countrymen, and the highest honors a great and free nation can accord, you will soon be permitted to return to your homes and families, conscious of having discharged the highest duty of American citizens. To achieve these glorious triumphs, and to secure to yourselves, fellow-countrymen and posterity, the blessings of free institutions, tens of thousands of your gallant comrades have fallen, and sealed the priceless legacy with their blood. The graves of these a grateful nation bedews with tears, honors their memories, and will ever cherish and support their stricken families."

General Lee's Generous Compliment to General Grant.

"I wish," said General R. E. Lee to a Northern friend, on one occasion, "to do simple justice to General Grant when I say that his treatment of the Army of Northern Virginia is without a parallel in the history of the civilized world. When my poor soldiers, with famished faces, had neither food nor raiment, General Grant immediately issued the humane order that 40,000 rations should be furnished to the impoverished troops. And that is not all. I was giving directions to one of my staff officers, when making out the list of things to be surrendered, to include the horses. At that moment, General Grant, who seemed to be paying no attention to what was transpiring, quickly said: 'No, no, General Lee, not a horse—not one—keep them all! Your people will need them for the Spring crops!'" "It was a scene never to be forgotten," adds the gentleman to whom the remarks were addressed, "to watch Lee's manner, when, with a spirit of chivalry equal to his skill and gallantry, he told, with moistened eyes, this and many other instances of the magnanimity so nobly displayed by his illustrious rival." Being subsequently asked who, in his opinion, was the greatest of the Federal commanders, General Lee paid the following handsome tribute to General Grant: "Both as a gentleman and an organizer of victorious war, General Grant has excelled all your most noted soldiers. He has exhibited more true courage, more real greatness of mind, more consummate prudence from the outset, and more heroic bravery than any one on your side."

AS PRESIDENT.

An Inaugural Extract.

In his address on the occasion of his inauguration for a second term as President, General Grant said:

It is my firm conviction that the civilized world is tending toward Republicanism, or government by the people through their chosen representatives, and that our own Republic is destined to be the guiding

CAPITOL AT WASHINGTON.

star. Under our Republic we support an army less than that of any European power of any standing, and a navy less than half that of at least five of them. * * * Now that the telegraph is made available for communicating thought, together with rapid transit by steam, all parts of the continent are made contiguous for all purposes of the government, and communication between the extreme limits of the country made easier than it was throughout the old Thirteen States at the beginning of our national existence.

President Grant—Closing Scenes in the White House—His Opinion of His Own Administration.

"The last time," says an intimate friend of the General, "that I saw the greatest man it has ever been my privilege to know was a week or so after President Hayes was inaugurated. Grant left the White House on the 5th of March, 1877. Hayes was inaugurated at 12 o'clock that day. About 2 o'clock, the outgoing and the incoming Presidents, attended by the outgoing Cabinet and a committee of Senators and Representatives, returned to the White House, when the man who had taken twice (on Sunday, the 4th, and on Monday, the 5th,) the oath to support the Constitution of the United States, and to well and truly perform the offices of Chief Magistrate, as God gave him light, took the reins of government from another man who had held them eight years, and was glad to lay them down.

"Mrs. Grant had provided an excellent lunch, and sat for the last time at the head of the Executive dining-room. After the lunch was over, she and 'that quiet man,' her husband, rode over to the residence of Hamilton Fish, Secretary of State, whose guests they were to be.

"Secretary Fish lived across the way from Fernando Wood and Blaine, at the corner of I and Fifteenth Streets, with his house fronting McPherson Square, one of those pleasant little irregular parks that make Washington so beautiful and purify the air we breathe. In it stands the statue of General McPherson, erected by the society of the Army of the Tennessee, with benches around it, upon which the tired tramp may rest.

"Strolling through this square one bright, warm morning in March, I found General Grant sitting upon one of the benches alone, with the historic cigar in his mouth and a newspaper upon his lap. He stopped me, and asked me to sit awhile and enjoy the sunshine with him. A cigar was offered and accepted, when the General chatted familiarly for half an hour.

"He talked of the events of his administration. He said some things not to be repeated, but the general drift of his opinion was that the country would be satisfied with it when it could be looked back upon, and the mischief-makers and discontented were pestering some one else. He thought that history would be charitable when it criticised his faults, and he knew that worse things than he had been charged with had been forgotten in the lives of his predecessors. That which he regretted most was the Bristow conspiracy, and he predicted that before many years Bristow would be a forgotten man. He spoke of the intimacy, which was then at its height, between President Hayes and the 'reformers' on the one hand, and the ex-Confederate leaders on the other, and prophesied that his successor, for whom he had great respect, would be led into serious trouble if he followed their advice. He had tried them all, he said, and they had given him stones for bread. They were selfish, impolitic, and unreasonable, and would be satisfied only so long as they could control. He had found that the safest men to advise with were Hamlin, Chandler, Morton, and others of their sort.

"While we were talking, a carriage drove up to the Fish mansion, and General Grant bade me good-by."

Off for Europe—General Grant's Good-Bye to Old Friends.

Previous to his departure for Europe General Grant spent several days in Philadelphia. The reception extended by the Quaker City was commensurate with its reputation for always doing the right thing in the best possible manner. General Grant was highly delighted, and at a farewell meeting said:

I had expected to make a speech to-day, and therefore can do nothing more than thank you, as I have had occasion to do so often within the past week. I have been only eight days in Philadelphia, and have been received with such unexpected kindness that it finds me with no words to thank you. What with driving in the park, and dinners afterward, and keeping it up until after midnight, and now to find myself still receiving your kind hospitality, I am afraid you have not left me stomach enough to cross the Atlantic.

This was followed by short and highly complimentary speeches from General Sherman, ex-Secretary Fish, ex-Secretary Chandler, ex-Secretary Robeson, ex-Senator Cameron, General Bailey, Governor Hartranft, and others; and so affected General Grant that he replied:

MY DEAR FRIENDS:—I was not aware that we would have so much speech-making here, or that it would be necessary for me to say any more to you, but I feel that the compliments you have so showered upon me were not altogether deserved—that they should not all be paid to me, either as a soldier or as a civil officer. As a general your praises do not all belong to me—as the executive of the nation they are not due to me. There is no man who can fill both or either of these positions without the help of good men. I selected my lieutenants when I was in both positions, and they were men, I believe, who could have filled my place often better than I did. I never flattered myself that I was entitled to the place you gave me. My lieutenants could have acted perhaps better than I, had the opportunity presented itself. Sherman could have taken my place, as a soldier or in a civil office, and so could Sheridan, and others I might name. I am sure if the country ever comes to this need again there will be men for the work. There will be men born for every emergency. Again I thank you, and again I bid you good-bye; and once again I say that, if I had failed, Sherman or Sheridan, or some of my other lieutenants, would have succeeded.

Soon after this the General was transferred to the "Indiana," and was off for Europe.

AROUND THE WORLD.

On a Foreign Shore—General Grant's Arrival In Liverpool—The Welcome Words—His Address In Manchester.

The "Indiana," with its celebrities, arrived in Liverpool May 28, making the trip in eleven days.

And now begins a series of magnificent "receptions," "banquetings," etc., which have followed General Grant around the world. From Liverpool to Chicago, in great cities and by the wayside, on mountain summits and down in the lowest "devels" of the "Comstock," everywhere the great General has been most heartily welcomed.

It is, perhaps, not too much to say, that no one in all history has received such personal homage, so spontaneous and genuine, as Ulysses S. Grant. It is true, in part, this has been representative and highly complimentary to our land and civilization, and yet, somehow, there attaches to Grant himself, in his quiet self poise, gentlemanly demeanor, due appreciation and heartfelt thankfulness, that we can not divorce the grand world-encircling chain of ovations from the *man* who has won a world-wide fame on the field of battle and in the honest discharge of duties in the highest office that a free people can anywhere bestow.

On his arrival at Liverpool, General Grant was welcomed by the Mayor in the following earnest and eloquent words:

"General Grant, I am proud that it has fallen to my lot as chief magistrate of Liverpool, to welcome to the shores

BANKS OF THE NILE.

of England so distinguished a citizen of the United States. You have, sir, stamped your name on the history of the world by your brilliant career as a soldier, and still more as a statesman, in the interests of peace.

"In the name of Liverpool, whose interests are so closely allied with your great country, I bid you hearty welcome, and I hope Mrs. Grant and yourself will enjoy your visit to old England."

General Grant left Liverpool May 30, for Manchester, where he was the guest of Mayor Heywood. At the Royal Exchange, in presence of a large assemblage of merchants, the General, in response to an address, said:

MR. MAYOR, MEMBERS OF THE COUNCIL OF MANCHESTER, LADIES AND GENTLEMEN:—It is scarcely possible for me to give utterance to the feelings called forth by the receptions which have been accorded me since my arrival in England. In Liverpool, where I spent a couple of days, I witnessed continuously the same interest that has been exhibited in the streets and in the public buildings of your city. It would be impossible for any person to have so much attention paid to him without feeling it, and it is impossible for me to give expression to the sentiments which have been evoked by it. I had intended upon my arrival in Liverpool to have hastened through to London, and from that city to visit the various points of interest in your country, Manchester being one of the most important among them. I am, and have been for many years, fully aware of the great amount of manufactures of Manchester, many of which find a market in my own country. I was very well aware, during the war, of the sentiments of the great mass of the people of Manchester toward the country to which I have the honor to belong, and also of the sentiments with regard to the struggle in which it fell to my lot to take a humble part. It was a great trial for us. For your expressions of sympathy at that time there exists a feeling of friendship toward Manchester distinct and separate from that which my countrymen also feel, and I trust always will feel, toward every part of

England. I therefore accept on the part of my country the compliments which have been paid to me as its representative, and thank you for them heartily.

General Grant's Reception in Salford and Leicester.

General Grant arrived in Salford May 31, and at a banquet spoke as follows:

"My reception since my arrival in England has been to me very expressive, and one for which I have to return thanks on behalf of my country.

"I can not help feeling that it is my country that is honored through me.

"It is the affection which the people of this island have for their children on the other side of the Atlantic, which they express to me as an humble representative of their offspring."

In Leicester, in response to an address of the mayor, magistrates, and others, General Grant said:

"Allow me, in behalf of my country and myself, to return you thanks for the honor, and for your kind reception, as well as for the other kind receptions which I have had since the time that I first landed on the soil of Great Britain.

"As children of this great commonwealth, we feel that you must have some reason to be proud of our great advancement since our separation from the mother country.

"I can assure you of our heartfelt good will, and express to you our thanks on behalf of the American people."

General Grant's Speech in London and Private Letter to a Friend in America, Describing His Travels.

General Grant arrived in London June 1, and after spending a time in visiting his daughter, Mrs. Sartoris, was, on the 15th of June, made an honorary citizen of London, and presented with the freedom of the city. This was made the occasion of a great reception, during which General Grant, in response to the address of the Chamberlain, said:

> It is a matter of some regret to me that I have never cultivated that art of public speaking which might have enabled me to express in suitable terms my gratitude for the compliment which has been paid to my countrymen and myself on this occasion. Were I in the habit of speaking in public, I should claim the right to express my opinion, and what I believe will be the opinion of my countrymen when the proceedings of this day shall have been telegraphed to them. For myself, I have been very much surprised at my reception at all places since the day I landed at Liverpool up to my appearance in this the greatest city of the world. It was entirely unexpected, and it is particularly gratifying to me. I believe that this honor is intended quite as much for the country which I have had the opportunity of serving in different capacities, as for myself, and I am glad that this is so, because I want to see the happiest relations existing, not only between the United States and Great Britain, but also between the United States and all other nations. Although a soldier by education and profession, I have never felt any sort of fondness for war, and I have never advocated it except as a means of peace. I hope that we shall always settle our differences in all future negotiations as amicably as we did in a recent instance. I believe that settlement has had a happy effect on both countries, and that from month to month, and year to year, the tie of common civilization and common blood is getting stronger between the two countries. My Lord Mayor, ladies and gentlemen, I again thank you for the honor you have done me and my country to-day.

THE OLD WORLD.

After this grand reception, on the following day General Grant wrote to his friend, George W. Childs, of Philadelphia, as follows:

"MY DEAR MR. CHILDS:—After an unusually stormy passage for any season of the year, and continuous sea-sickness generally among the passengers after the second day out, we reached Liverpool Monday afternoon, the 28th of May. Jesse and I proved to be among the few good sailors. Neither of us felt a moment's uneasiness during the voyage.

"I had proposed to leave Liverpool immediately on arrival, and proceed to London, where I knew our Minister had made arrangements for a formal reception, and had accepted for me a few invitations of courtesy; but what was my surprise to find nearly all the shipping in port at Liverpool decorated with flags of all nations, and from the mainmast of each the flag of the Union was most conspicuous.

"The docks were lined with as many of the population as could find standing room, and the streets, to the hotel where it was understood my party would stop, were packed. The demonstration was, to all appearances, as hearty and as enthusiastic as at Philadelphia on our departure.

"The Mayor was present, with his state carriage, to convey us to the hotel, and after that to his beautiful country residence, some six miles out, where we were entertained at dinner with a small party of gentlemen, and remained over night. The following day a large party was given at the official residence of the Mayor, in the city, at which there were some one hundred and fifty of the distinguished citizens and officers of the corporation present. Pressing invitations were sent from most of the cities of the kingdom to have me visit them. I accepted for a day at Manchester, and stopped a few moments at Leicester, and at one other place. The same hearty welcome was shown at each place, as you have no doubt seen.

"The press of the country has been exceedingly kind and courteous. So far I have not been permitted to travel in a regular train, much less in a common car. The Midland road, which penetrates a great portion of the island, including Wales and Scotland, have extended to me the courtesy of their road, and a Pullman car to take me wherever I wish to go during the whole of my stay in England. We arrived in London on Monday evening, the 30th of May, when I found our Minister had accepted engagements for me up to the 27th of June, having but a few spare days in the interval.

"On Saturday last we dined with the Duke of Wellington, and last night the formal reception at Judge Pierrepont's was held. It was a great success, most brilliant in the numbers, rank, and attire of the audience, and was graced by the presence of every American in the city who had called on the minister or left a card for me. I doubt whether London has ever seen a private house so elaborately or tastefully decorated as was our American minister's last night. I am deeply indebted to him for the pains he has taken to make my stay pleasant, and the attentions extended to our country. I appreciate the fact, and am proud of it, that the attentions I am receiving are intended more for our country than for me personally. I love to see our country honored and respected abroad, and I am proud to believe that it is by most all nations, and by some even loved. It has always been my desire to see all jealousy between England and the United States abated, and every sore healed. Together they are more powerful for the spread of commerce and civilization than all others combined, and can do more to remove causes of wars by creating moral interests that would be so much endangered by war.

"I have written very hastily, and a good deal at length, but I trust this will not bore you. Had I written for publication, I should have taken more pains.

"U. S. GRANT."

General Grant's Celebrated Liverpool Speech.

In his second visit to Liverpool, June 28, at a banquet, General Grant made one of his longest and most happy speeches. It was as follows:

MR. MAYOR AND GENTLEMEN:—You have alluded to the hearty reception given to me on my first landing on the soil of Great Britain, and the expectations of the Mayor that this reception would be equaled throughout the island have been more than realized. It has been far beyond anything I could have expected. (Cheers.) I am a soldier, and the gentlemen here beside me know that a soldier must die. I have been a President, but we know that the term of the presidency expires, and when it has expired he is no more than a dead soldier. (Laughter and cheers.) But, gentlemen, I have met with a reception that would have done honor to any living person. (Cheers.) I feel, however, that the compliment has been paid, not to me, but to my country. I can not help but at this moment being highly pleased at the good feeling and good sentiment which now exist between the two peoples who of all others should be good friends. We are of one kindred, of one blood, of one language, and of one civilization, though in some respects we believe that we, being younger, surpass the mother country. (Laughter.) You have made improvements on the soil and the surface of the earth which we have not yet done, but which we do not believe will take us as long as it took you. (Laughter and applause.) I heard some military remarks which impressed me a little at the time—I am not quite sure whether they were in favor of the volunteers or against them. I can only say from my own observation that you have as many troops at Aldershott as we have in the whole of our regular army, notwithstanding we have many thousands of miles of frontier to guard and hostile Indians to control. But if it became necessary to raise a volunteer force, I do not think we could do better than follow your example. General Fairchild and myself are examples of volunteers who came forward when their assistance was necessary, and I have no doubt that if you ever needed such services, you would have support from your reserve forces and volunteers far more effective than you can conceive. (Cheers.)

Queen Victoria and General Grant at Dinner—A Very Happy Affair.

The Queen of England paid a compliment to General Grant and the United States by extending him and his family an invitation to visit Windsor Castle.

The invitation read as follows:

"'The Lord Steward of Her Majesty's household is commanded by the Queen to invite Mr. and Mrs. Grant to dinner at Windsor Castle, on Wednesday, the 27th inst., and to remain until the following day, the 28th of June, 1877." Invitations were also extended to Mr. Pierrepont and his wife, J. R. Grant and General Badeau. On the 26th of June the party left for Windsor by the afternoon train.

At half-past eight, the Queen, surrounded by her court, received General Grant in the magnificent corridor leading to her private apartments in the Quadrangle. The Quadrangle is formed by the state apartments on the north, the historical Round Tower on the west, and the private apartments of the Queen and the royal household on the south and east.

This corridor is 520 feet long, and extends round the south and east sides of the Quadrangle. The ceiling, which is lofty, is divided into large squares, the centers of which bear a number of ornamental devices, typical of ancient, modern and ecclesiastical history. The dinner was served in the Oak Room. Among those present were Prince Leopold, Prince Christian, Princess Beatrice, Lord and Lady Derby, the Duchess of, Wellington, General Badeau, and others.

The ladies were dressed in black with white trimmings, owing to the recent decease of the Queen of Holland. During the dinner a dispatch was received from Governor Hartranft, of Pennsylvania, as follows:

154   STORIES AND SKETCHES OF GEN. GRANT.

To GENERAL U. S. GRANT, *care of* H. M. THE QUEEN:—Your comrades, in national encampment assembled, in Rhode Island, send heartiest greetings to their old commander, and desire, through England's Queen, to thank England for Grant's reception.

To this the General responded:

Grateful for telegram. Conveyed message to the Queen. Thank my old comrades.

The dispatch came just as the party were assembling for dinner, and was given by the General to Her Majesty, who expressed much pleasure at the kind greeting from America. During the dinner the band of the Grenadier Guards played in the Quadrangle.

After dinner the Queen entered into conversation with the party, and about ten took her leave, followed by her suite. The evening was given to conversation and whist, with members of the royal household, and at half-past eleven they retired.

The next morning the General and party took their leave of Windsor and returned to London.

Address of General Grant to the Workingmen.

On the 3d of July, at the house of General Badeau, General Grant received a deputation of the leading representatives of the workingmen of London and the provinces, representing the engineers, iron-founders, miners, and other classes of industry. An address, handsomely engrossed on vellum, was read by Mr. Guile, of the Iron Founders' Society. General Grant replied as follows:

" In the name of my country, I thank you for the address you have presented to me. I feel it a great compliment paid my government, and one to me personally. Since my arrival on British soil I have received great attentions, which were intended, I feel sure, in the same way, for my country. I have had ovations, free hand-shakings, presentations from different classes, from the government, from the controlling authorities of cities, and have been received in the cities by the populace, but there has been no reception which I am prouder of than this to-day. I recognize the fact that whatever there is of greatness in the United States, as indeed in any other country, is due to labor. The laborer is the author of all greatness and wealth. Without labor there would be no government, or no leading class, or nothing to preserve. With us, labor is regarded as highly respectable. When it is not so regarded, it is because man dishonors labor. We recognize that labor dishonors no man; and, no matter what a man's occupation is, he is eligible to fill any post in the gift of the people; his occupation is not considered in selecting, whether as a law-maker or as an executor of the law. Now, gentlemen, in conclusion, all I can do is to renew my thanks for the address, and repeat what I have said before, that I have received nothing from any class since my arrival which has given me more pleasure."

After the speech there was an informal exchange of courtesies, and the deputation then withdrew.

General Grant in Paris.

The month of October finds General Grant in Paris, where he greatly enjoyed the magnificence of that famous city. Notre Dame was an object of special interest, which after St. Peter's at Rome is the grandest church edifice in the world.

Sight-seeing was, however, interrupted from time to time by the numerous attentions and civilities showered on General Grant. On the 29th of October, General Noyes, the American Minister, gave the Ex-President a reception at his house on the Avenue Josephine. This reception was of the most brilliant character, and was attended by all the leading Americans in Paris. None of the Republican leaders were, however, present. Subsequently, Mr. Healey, the artist, arranged a meeting, at which General Grant met M. Gambetta. From this and other meetings, a high feeling of esteem arose for the French Republican leader, who impressed the General as one of the foremost minds in Europe. It was on the 6th of November that the members of the American colony, numbering some three hundred, gave a public dinner to General Grant at the Grand Hotel. With but few exceptions, every American in Paris was present. General Noyes presided, and among the guests were MM. Rochambeau and Lafayette, the latter descended from the Revolutionary hero of that name. The veteran journalist, Emile Girardin, was there, whom Horace Greeley called the greatest journalist in the world. Edmond About and Laboulaye were present. This dinner proceeded without special incident, the General being received with the greatest enthusiasm, and making a brief speech. These two dinners, with one at the Elyseés, were the special events of the General's visit. General Torbert entertained the Ex-President at his apartment. On the 20th of November, Madame Mackey, of California, gave a reception at her house near the Arch of Triumph, which, from its splendor, recalled scenes in the "Arabian Nights."

Ascending Mt. Vesuvius.

While visiting the beautiful city of Naples, General Grant, John Russell Young, and others, made the ascent of Mt. Vesuvius. Mr. Young has given a graphic description of the extensive "climb," as follows:

"There, far above, was Vesuvius, and we were impatient

NAPLES.

for the ascent. It was too late when we arrived in Naples, but the General, with military promptness, gave orders for the march next morning. We stood on the deck and studied the stern old mountain, and picked out the various objects with a telescope, and did an immense amount of reading on the subject. The volcano was in a lazy mood, and not alive to the honor of a visit from the Ex-President of the United States, for all he deigned to give us was a lazy puff of smoke, not a spark, or a flame, or a cinder. I suppose the old monster is an aristocrat, and a conservative, and said: 'What do I care for presidents, or your new republics! I have scattered my ashes over a Roman republic. I have lighted Cæsar's triumphs, and thrown my clouds over the path of Brutus fresh from Cæsar's corpse. Why should I set my forces in motion to please a party of Yankee sight-seers, even if one of them should be a famous general and ex-ruler of a republic? I have looked upon Hannibal and Cæsar, Charlemagne and Bonaparte. I have seen the rise and fall of empires. I have admonished generations who have worshiped Jupiter, as I have admonished generations who have worshiped the Cross. I am the home of the gods; and if you would see my power, look at my base and ask of the ashes that cumber Herculaneum and Pompeii.' So the stubborn old monster never gave us a flash of welcome, only a smoky puff now and then to tell us that he was a monster all the time, if he only chose to manifest his awful will. We stood upon the deck in speculation, and some of us hoped that there would be an eruption or something worth describing. The General was bent on climbing to the very summit and looking into the crater, and with that purpose we started on the morning of Tuesday, December 18th.

"We should have gone earlier, but many high people in uniforms, commanding one thing or another, had to come on board and pay their respects. It was ten before we were under way, the General and party in the advance, with our courier, whom we have called the Marquis, on the box, and Mrs. Grant's maid bringing up the rear. We drove all the way.

"Vesuvius is now a double mountain upon an extended base from thirty to forty miles in circumference, not more than one third the base of Etna. Its height varies. In 1868 it was 4,255 feet; but since 1872 it has slightly diminished. Stromboli is 3,022 feet, but, although in constant motion, the stones nearly all fall back into the crater. Etna is 10,870 feet in height, but slopes so gradually, and has so broad a base, that it looks more like a table land than a mountain. I did not see Stromboli, for although we sailed near it, the mist and rain hid it from view. I have seen Etna, however, and think it far less imposing and picturesque than Vesuvius.

"In the meantime we are going up steadily. The horses go slower and slower. Some of us get out and help them by walking part of the way and taking short cuts. The few houses that we see on the roadside have evidently been built with a view to eruptions, for the roofs are made of heavy stone and cement. General Grant notes that where the lava and stones have been allowed to rest and to mingle with the soil, good crops spring up, and here and there we note a flourishing bit of vineyard. Soon, however, vineyards disappear, and after the vineyards the houses, except an occasional house of shelter, into which we are all invited to enter and drink of the Tears of Christ.

"Still we climb the hill, going steadily up. Those of us who thought we could make the way on foot repent, for the way is steep and the road is hard. All around us is an ocean of chaos and death. There in all forms and shapes lie the lava streams that did their work in other days, black and cold and forbidding. You can trace the path of each eruption as distinctly as the windings of the stream from the mountain top. We are now high up on the mountain, and beneath us is the valley and the Bay of Naples, with Ischia and Capri, and on the other horizon a range of mountains tinged and tipped with snow. In one direction we see the eruption of 1872; the black lava stream bordered with green. What forms and shapes! what fantastic, horrible shapes the fire assumed in the hours of its triumph! I can well see how Martial and Virgil and the early poets saw in these phenomena the strife and anger of the gods. Virgil describes Enceladus transfixed by Jove and the mountain thrown upon him, which shakes and trembles whenever he turns his weary sides. This is the scene, the very scene of his immortal agony. There are no two forms alike; all is black, cold, and pitiless. If we could only see one living thing in this mass of destruction; but all is death, all desolation. Here and there, where the rains have washed the clay, and the birds, perhaps, may have carried seed, the grass begins to grow; but the whole scene is desolation. I thought of the earlier ages, when the earth was black and void, and fancied that it was just such an earth as this when Divinity looked upon it and said, "Let there be light." I thought of the end of all things, of our earth, our fair, sweet and blooming earth, again a mass of lava, rock and ashes, all life gone out of it, rolling through space.

"The presence of a phenomenon like this, and right above us the ever-seething crater, is in itself a solemn and beautiful sight. We all felt repaid with our journey; for by this time we had come to the journey's end, and our musings upon eternity and chaos did not forbid thoughts of luncheon. For the wind was cold and we were hungry. So when our illustrious captain intimated that we might seek a place of refuge and entertainment, a light gleamed in the eyes of the Marquis, and he reined us up at a hostelry called the Hermitage.

" There, in quite a primitive fashion, we had our luncheon, helping ourselves and each other in good homely American fashion, for we were as far from the amenities of civilization as though we were in Montana.

" After luncheon we walked about, looking at the crater, where fumes were quite apparent—at the world of desolation around us, some of it centuries old, but as fresh and terrible as when it burst from the world of fire beneath us. But there was still another picture—one of sublime and marvelous beauty. There beneath us, in the clear, sunny air—there was Naples, queen among cities, and her villages clustering about her. Beautiful, wondrously beautiful, that panorama of hill and field and sea, that rolled before us thousands of feet below! We could count twenty villages in the plain, their white roofs massed together and spangling the green plain like gems."

In Egypt.

General Grant arrived in Egypt early in January, 1878. The Khedive gave him a palace in the suburbs of the capital—an Oriental building, with a French decoration and furniture—and sent him up the Nile in his own yacht. General Grant made the fastest Nile trip on record. He went as far as the first cataract, the Island of Philae, visiting Thebes, Abidos, the Pyramids, and Memphis, and what added to the interest of the visit was that the Khedive sent with the party perhaps the most distinguished Egyptian scholar living, Brugsch, a most accomplished man, who knew hieroglyphics as well as he knew his own language, and made everything plain to the company.

"What a blank our trip would be without Brugsch," said the General one day, as the party were coming back from a ruin. John Russell Young, who accompanied General Grant up the Nile describes the journey and pastimes as follows:

"We breakfast whenever we please—in the French fashion. The General is an early or late riser, according as we have an engagement for the day. If there are ruins to be seen in the morning, he is generally first on the deck with his Indian helmet swathed in silk, and as he never waits, we are off on military time. If there are no sights to be seen, the morning hours drift away. We lounge on the deck. We go among the Arabs and see them cooking. We lean over the prow and watch the sailors poke the Nile with long poles and call out the message from its bed. Sometimes a murderous feeling steals over some of the younger people, and they begin to shoot at a stray crane or pelican. I am afraid these shots do not diminish the resources of the Nile, and the General suggests that the sportsmen go ashore and fire at the poor, patient, drudging

camel, who pulls his heavy-laden hump along the bank. There are long pauses of silence, in which the General maintains his long-conceded supremacy. Then come little ripples of real, useful conversation, when the General strikes some theme connected with the war or his administration. Then one wishes that he might gather up and bind these sheaves of history. Or perhaps our friend Brugsch opens upon some theme connected with Egypt. And we sit in grateful silence while he tells us of the giants who reigned in the old dynasties, of the gods they honored, of the tombs and temples, of their glory and their fall. I think that we will all say that the red-letter hours of our Nile journey were when General Grant told us how he met Lee at Appomattox, or how Sherman fought at Shiloh, or when Brugsch, in a burst of fine enthusiasm, tells us of the glories of the eighteenth dynasty, or what Karnak must have been in the days of its splendors and its pride. But you must not suppose that we have nothing but serious talk in those idle hours on the Nile."

At Pompeii.

It is said that General Grant, in speaking of his journey abroad, stated that " Pompeii was one of the few things which had not disappointed his expectations; that the truth was more striking than the imagination had painted," and that " it was worth a journey over the sea to see and study its stately, solemn ruins."

The Italian authorities did General Grant special honor on his visit to this place by directing that a house should be excavated. It is one of the special compliments paid to visitors of renown. Houses are shown, by the guide, that have been excavated in the presence of Murat and his queen, of Joseph II, Admiral Farragut, and General Sher-

DEPARTED GLORY.

man, and General Sheridan. These houses are still known by the names of the illustrious persons who witnessed their excavation.

General Grant's visit was known only to a few. The quarter selected was near the Forum. Chairs were arranged for the General, Mrs. Grant, and some of us, and there quietly, in a room that had known Pompeiian life seventeen centuries ago, we awaited the signal that was to dig up the ashes that had fallen from Vesuvius that terrible night in August. Our group was composed of the General, his wife and son, Mr. Duncan, the American Consul in Naples, Commander Robeson, of the "Vandalia," Lieutenants Strong, Miller and Rush, and Engineer Baird, of the same ship. We formed a group about the General, while the director gave the workmen the signal. The spades dived into the ashes, while with eager eyes we looked on. What story would be revealed of that day of agony and death? Perhaps a mother, almost in the fruition of a proud mother's hopes, lying in the calm repose of centuries, like the figure we had seen only an hour ago dug from these very ruins. Perhaps a miser hurrying with his coin only to fall in his doorway, there to rest in peace while seventeen centuries of the mighty world rolled over him, and to end at last in a museum. Perhaps a soldier fallen at his post, or a reveler stricken at the feast. All these things have been given us from Pompeii, and we stood watching the nimble spades and the tumbling ashes, watching with the greedy eyes of gamblers to see what chance would send. Nothing came of any startling import. There were two or three bronze ornaments, a loaf of bread wrapped in cloth, the grain of the bread and the fiber of the cloth as clearly marked as when the probable remnant of an humble meal was put aside by the careful housewife's hands. Beyond this, and some fragments

which we could not understand, this was all that came from the excavation of Pompeii. The director was evidently disappointed. He expected a skeleton at the very least to come out of the cruel ashes and welcome our renowned guest, who had come so many thousand miles to this Roman entertainment. He proposed to open another ruin, but one of our " Vandalia " friends, a very practical gentleman, remembered that it was cold, and that he had been walking a good deal and was hungry, and when he proposed that, instead of excavating another ruin, we should " excavate a beefsteak " at the restaurant near the gate of the sea, there was an approval. The General, who had been leisurely smoking his cigar and studying the scene with deep interest, quietly assented, and thanking the director for his courtesy, said he would give him no more trouble.

In Constantinople.

Constantinople as seen from the Bosphorus is the most beautiful city in the world. When you land, however, all the illusion passes away.

The Turks were very kind to General Grant. The Sultan, although he was at the time of the General's visit in the agony of signing a treaty of humiliation and dismemberment for his country, showed him great attention. General Grant did not visit the Russian headquarters, although he was anxious to do so. He thought, however, that having been the guest of the Sultan to a certain extent, it would be ungracious for him to go from the palace of his host to the headquarters of a conquering army encamped in the suburbs of the capital.

There was some criticism at the time, some censure of General Grant for what was an apparent discourtesy in not

CONSTANTINOPLE.

visiting the Russian army, but the thing was talked over at the time, and the General decided not to go, out of consideration for the feelings of his hosts. He preferred to see the Russians in Russia.

Many excursions were made to the various palaces built by the recent predecessors of the present Sultan, who all seemed to have had a mania for building costly edifices, quite indifferent as to where the money came from.

Some of the party, with antiquarian zeal, visited the great Hippodrome, which once was the rival of the Roman Coliseum.

One thing which General Grant observed as being peculiar in Constantinople was its quiet after a certain hour at night. By half-past nine, there are no moving figures in the streets, save that of an occasional patrol of soldiers going to the relief of a post.

In Jerusalem.

General Grant's visit to the Holy Land is said to have been exceedingly interesting, though the party was unfortunate so far as the weather was concerned. The heaviest snow storm which had fallen in twelve years greeted the General on his arrival, but, notwithstanding, his reception was enthusiastic.

We had expected, says Mr. Young, to enter Jerusalem in our quiet, plain way, pilgrims really coming to see the Holy City, awed by its renowned memories.

But lo and behold! Here is an army with banners, and we are commanded to enter as conquerors, in a triumphal manner! Well, I know of one in that company who looked with sorrow upon the pageantry, and he it was for whom it was intended.

JEPHTHAH'S VOW.

The General had just been picturing to his companions what a pleasant thing it would be to reach Jerusalem about five, to go to our hotel, and stroll around quietly and see the town. There would be no palaces, or soldiers, or ceremonies, such as had honored and oppressed us in Egypt. But the General had scarcely drawn this picture of what his fancy hoped would await him in the Holy City, when the horsemen came galloping out of the rain and mist, and told us we were expected.

Well, there was no help for it, for there were cavalry, and the music, and the dragomans of all nations, in picturesque costumes, and the American flag floating, and our Consul, the proudest man in Palestine.

Arrived at the city, General Grant was at once called upon by the Pacha and the Consuls. The Bishops and the Patriarchs all came and blessed the General and his house. The Pacha sent his band of fifty pieces in the evening to serenade the ex-President. The Pacha also gave a state dinner, which was largely attended.

Early the following morning General Grant stole away, before the reception ceremonies, and walked over the street Via Dolorosa, consecrated to Christianity as the street over which Jesus carried His cross. The General lived, while in Jerusalem, within five minutes' walk of Calvary, and with this sacred mount in plain sight from his window.

General Grant and Prince Bismarck—An Interesting Interview between Two Remarkably Great Men.

Soon after General Grant's arrival in Berlin, he called upon Prince Bismarck, going to the palace alone and on foot. As he passes into the court-yard, the sentinels present arms, and the General raises his hat in honor of the salute. The doors are opened, and the Prince, taking the General by the hand, said:

"Glad to welcome General Grant to Germany."

The General answered that there, was no incident in his German visit that more interested him than this opportunity of meeting the Prince.

Bismarck expressed surprise at seeing the General so young a man, but on a comparison of ages it was found that Bismarck was only eleven years the General's senior.

"That," said the Prince, "shows the value of a military life; for here you have the frame of a young man, while I feel like an old man."

The General, smiling, announced that he was at that period of life when he could have no higher compliment than being called a young man. By this time the Prince had escorted the General to a chair.

It was his library or study, and an open window looked out upon a beautiful park, upon which the warm June sun was shining. This is the private park of the Radziwill Palace, which is now Bismarck's Berlin home. The library is a large, spacious room, the walls a gray marble, and the furniture plain. In one corner is a large and high writing-desk, where the Chancellor works, and on the varnished floors a few rugs are thrown.

The Prince speaks English with precision, but slowly, as though lacking in practice, now and then taking refuge in a French word, but showing a thorough command of the language.

CATHEDRAL AT STRASSBURG.

After inquiring after the health of General Sheridan, who was a fellow-campaigner in France, and became a great friend of Bismarck's, they discussed the Eastern question, military armament and strength, and the late atrocious attempt to assassinate the Emperor, giving the two great men an opportunity to discuss this phase of socialism. In speaking of this attempt on the life of the Emperor, the Prince paid the following glowing tribute to the Emperor:

"It is so strange, so strange and so sad. Here is an old man—one of the kindest old gentlemen in the world—and yet they must try and shoot him! There never was a more simple, more genuine, more—what shall I say?—more humane character than the Emperor's. He is totally unlike men born in his station, or many of them, at least. You know that men who come into the world in his rank, born princes, are apt to think themselves of another race and another world. They are apt to take small account of the wishes and feelings of others. All their education tends to deaden the human side. But this Emperor is so much of a man in all things! He never did any one a wrong in his life. He never wounded any one's feelings; never imposed a hardship! He is the most genial and winning of men—thinking always, anxious always for the comfort and welfare of his people, of those around him. You can not conceive a finer type of the noble, courteous, charitable old gentleman, with every high quality of a prince, as well as every virtue of a man. I should have supposed that the Emperor could have walked alone all over the Empire without harm, and yet they must try and shoot him."

The Prince asked the General when he might have the pleasure of seeing Mrs. Grant. The General answered that she would receive him at any convenient hour.

"Then," said the Prince, "I will come to-morrow before the Congress meets."

Both gentlemen arose, and the General renewed the expression of his pleasure at having seen a man who was so well known and so highly esteemed in America.

"General," answered the Prince, "the pleasure and the honor are mine. Germany and America have always been in so friendly a relation that nothing delights us more than to meet Americans, and especially an American who has done so much for his country, and whose name is so much honored in Germany as your own."

The Prince and the General walked side by side to the door, and after shaking hands the General passed into the square. The guard presented arms, and the General lit a fresh cigar and slowly strolled home.

"I am glad I have seen Bismarck," he remarked. "He is a man whose manner and bearing fully justify the opinions one forms of him. What he says about the Emperor was beautifully said, and should be known to all the Germans and those who esteem Germany."

In Edinburgh.

After a "run to the Continent," General Grant returned to the "English Speaking" realm of the old world, and in reply to the Lord Provost's speech at Edinburgh, in Scotland, said:

I am so filled with emotion that I hardly know how to thank you for the honor conferred upon me by making me a burgess of this ancient city of Edinburgh. I feel that it is a great compliment to me and to my country. Had I eloquence I might dwell somewhat on the history of the great men you have produced, or the numerous citizens of this city and

Scotland that have gone to America, and the record they have made. We are proud of Scotchmen as citizens of America. They make good citizens of our country, and they find it profitable to themselves. (Laughter.) I again thank you for the honor you have conferred upon me.

Grant's Speech in Glasgow.

General Grant visited Glasgow September 13, where he was warmly received. The usual reception followed, where Grant made the following eloquent speech:

I rise to thank you for the great honor that has been conferred upon me this day by making me a free burgess of this great city of Glasgow. The honor is one that I shall cherish, and I shall always remember this day.

When I am back in my own country, I will be able to refer with pride not only to my visit to Glasgow, but to all the different towns in this kingdom that I have had the pleasure and the honor of visiting. (Applause.)

I find that I am being made so much a citizen of Scotland, it will become a serious question where I shall go to vote. (Laughter and applause.) You have railroads and other facilities for getting from one place to another, and I might vote frequently in Scotland by starting early. I do not know how you punish that crime over here; it is a crime that is very often practiced by people who come to our country and become citizens there by adoption. In fact, I think they give the majority of the votes. I do not refer to Scotchmen particularly, but to naturalized citizens.

But to speak more seriously, ladies and gentlemen, I feel the honor of this occasion, and I beg to thank you, ladies and gentlemen of this city of Glasgow, for the kind words of your Lord Provost, and for the kind expression of this audience.

Speech at Newcastle.

The following address was in reply to the remarks by the President of the Newcastle Chamber of Commerce:

The President in his remarks has alluded to the personal friendship existing between the two nations—I will not say the two peoples, because we are one people (applause); but we are two nations having a common destiny, and that destiny will be brilliant in proportion to the friendship and co-operation of the brethren on the two sides of the water. (Applause.)

During my eight years of Presidency, it was my study to heal up all the sores that were existing between us. (Applause.) That healing was accomplished in a manner honorable to the nations. (Applause.) From that day to this feelings of amity have been constantly growing, as I think; I know it has been so on our side, and I believe never to be disturbed again.

These are two nations which ought to be at peace with each other. We ought to strive to keep at peace with all the world besides (applause), and by our example stop those wars which have devastated our own countries, and are now devastating some countries in Europe.

"Let us Have Peace."

Before one of the English societies, organized in the interest of peace, the General made the following speech:

MEMBERS OF THE MIDLAND INTERNATIONAL ARBITRATION UNION:— I thank you for your address. It is one that gives me very little to reply to, more than to express my thanks. Though I have followed a military life for the better part of my years, there was never a day of my life when I was not in favor of peace on any terms that were honorable.

It has been my misfortune to be engaged in more battles than any other general on the other side of the Atlantic; but there was never a time during my command that I would not have gladly chosen some settlement by reason rather than by the sword.

I am conscientiously, and have been from the beginning, an advocate of what the society represented by you, gentlemen, is seeking to carry out; and nothing would afford me greater happiness than to know, as I believe to be the case, that, at some future day, the nations of the earth will agree upon some sort of congress, which shall take cognizance of international questions of difficulty, and whose decisions will be as binding as the decision of our Supreme Court is binding on us.

It is a dream of mine that some such solution may be found for all questions of difficulty that may arise between different nations. In one of the addresses, I have forgotten which, reference was made to the dismissal of the army to the pursuits of peaceful industry.

1 would gladly see the millions of men who are now supported by the industry of the nations return to industrial pursuits, and thus become self-sustaining, and take off the tax upon labor which is now levied for their support.

Address to the Working People.

The address of the General at Tyneside, in behalf of the workingmen, was prefaced by some eloquent remarks of Mr. Burt, M. P., the closing words of which were as follows:

"And now, General, in our final words we greet you as a sincere friend of labor. Having attested again and again your deep solicitude for the industrial classes, and having also nobly proclaimed the dignity of labor by breaking the chains of the slave, you are entitled to our sincere and unalloyed gratitude; and our parting wish is, that the general applause which you have received in your own country, and are now receiving in this, for the many triumphs which you have so gloriously achieved, may be succeeded by a peaceful repose, and that the sunset of your life may be attended with all the blessings that this earth can afford."

General Grant then arose and delivered one of his longest and best speeches. It was as follows:

"Mr. Burt and Workingmen:—Through you I will return thanks to the workingmen of Tyneside for the very acceptable welcome address which you have just read. I accept from that class of people the reception which they have accorded me, as among the most honorable. We all know that but for labor we would have very little that is worth fighting for, and when wars do come they fall upon the many, the producing class, who are the sufferers. They not only have to furnish the means largely, but they have, by their labor and industry, to produce the means for those who are engaged in destroying and not in producing.

"I was always a man of peace, and I have always advocated peace, although educated a soldier. I never willingly, although I have gone through two wars, of my own accord advocated war. (Loud cheers.)

"I advocated what I believed to be right, and I have fought for it to the best of my ability in order that an honorable peace might be secured. You have been pleased to allude to the friendly relations existing between the two great nations on both sides of the Atlantic. They are now most friendly, and the friendship has been increasing.

"Our interests are so identified, we are so much related to each other, that it is my sincere hope, and it has been the sincere hope of my life, and especially of my official life, to maintain that friendship. I entertain views of the progress to be made in the future by the union and friendship of the great English-speaking people, for I believe that it will result in the spread of our language, our civilization, and our industry, and be for the benefit of mankind generally. (Cheers.)

"I do not know, Mr. Burt, that there is anything more for me to say, except that I would like to communicate to the people whom I see assembled before me here this day, how greatly I feel the honor which they have conferred upon me." (Cheers.)

Speech in Sheffield—Grant's First Penknife.

General Grant visited Sheffield on the 20th of September. The town was decorated, and the General arrived on the Pullman palace car. He drove to the Cutlers' Hall. The aldermen were present in scarlet, and the councilors in purple. In the center of the platform three chairs were reserved for the Mayor, the General, and Mrs. Grant. The Mayor welcomed the General to Sheffield, and an address was read in which America was congratulated on having abolished slavery. In his response the General said:

MR. MAYOR, LADIES AND GENTLEMEN OF SHEFFIELD:—I have just heard the address which has been read and presented to me, with great gratification. It affords me singular pleasure to visit a city the name of which has been familiar to me from my earliest childhood. I think the first penknife I ever owned, away out in the western part of the State of Ohio, was marked "Sheffield." I think the knives and forks we then used on our table had all of them "Sheffield" marked on them. I do not know whether they were counterfeit or not, but it gave them a good market. From that day to this the name of your industrial city has been familiar, not only in the States, but I suppose throughout the civilized world. The city has been distinguished for its industry, its inventions, and its progress. If our commerce has not increased as much as you might wish, yet it has increased, I think, with Sheffield since the days of which I spoke when we had no cutlery excepting that marked "Sheffield." It must be very much larger than it was then. We are getting to make some of those things ourselves, and I believe occasionally we put our own stamp upon them; but Sheffield cutlery still has a high place in the markets of the world. I assure you the welcome I have received here to-day affords me very great pleasure, and I shall carry away with me the pleasant recollections of what I have seen in Sheffield.

General Grant's Great Speech in Birmingham.

"MR. MAYOR, LADIES AND GENTLEMEN OF BIRMINGHAM:—I scarcely know how to respond to a toast which has been presented in such eloquent language, and in terms so complimentary to myself and to the nation to which I belong, and in which I have had the honor of holding a public position. There are some few points, however, alluded to by your representative in Parliament, that I will respond to. He alluded to the great merit of retiring a large army at the close of a great war. If he had ever been in my position for four years, and undergone all the anxiety and care that I had in the management of those large armies, he would appreciate how happy I was to be able to say that they could be dispensed with. (Laughter and applause.) I disclaim all credit and praise for doing that one thing.

"I knew that I was doomed to become a citizen of the United States, and, so far as my personal means went, to aid in ;eradicating the debt already created, and in paying my share of any expenses that might have to be borne for the support of a large standing army.

"Then, further, we Americans claim to be so much of Englishmen, and to have so much general intelligence, and so much personal independence and individuality, that we do not quite believe that it is possible for any one man there to assume any more right and authority than the constitution of the land gave to him. (Hear, hear.) Among the English-speaking people we do not think these things possible.

"We can fight among ourselves, and dispute and abuse each other, but we will not allow ourselves to be abused outside; nor will those who look on at our little personal quarrels in our own midst permit us to interfere with their own rights. Now, there is one subject that has been alluded to here that I do not know that I should speak upon it at all; I have heard it occasionally whispered since I have been in England —and that is, the [great advantages that would accrue to the United States if free trade should only be established.

"I have a sort of recollection, through reading, that England herself had a protective tariff until she had manufactories somewhat established. I think we are rapidly progressing in the way of establishing manufactories ourselves, and I believe we shall become one of the greatest free-trade nations on the face of the earth; and when we both come to be free-traders, I think that probably the balance of nations had better stand aside, and not contend with us at all in the markets of the world.

"If I had been accustomed to public speaking—I never did speak in public in my life until I came to England—I would respond further to this toast; but I believe that the better policy would be to thank you not only for the toast, and the language in which it has been presented, but for the very gratifying reception which I have had personally in Birmingham."

Speech in Brighton.

In response to the Mayor's address of welcome, the General said:

"MR. MAYOR AND GENTLEMEN:—I have to rise here in answer to a toast that has made it embarrassing to me, by the very complimentary terms in which it has been proposed. But I can say to you all, gentlemen, that since my arrival in England, I have had the most agreeable receptions everywhere; and I enjoy yours exceedingly.

"In a word, I will say that Brighton has advantages which very few places have, in consequence of its proximity to the greatest city in the world. There you can go and transact your business, and return in the evening.

"If I were an Englishman, I think I should select Brighton as a place where I should live, and I am very sure you could not meet a jollier and better people anywhere. But I would say one word in regard to a toast which preceded, and that is in regard to your Forces. I must say one word for the Volunteers, or Reserve Forces, as I believe you call them. They are what the English-speaking people are to rely on in the future. I believe that wherever there is a great war between one civilized nation and another, it will be these Forces in which they will have to place their confidence.

"We English-speaking people keep up the public schools in order to maintain and advance the intelligence of our country, and, in time, fit our people for volunteer service, and for higher training; and you will always find the men among them who are equal to any occasion. I have forgotten a good deal your Mayor has said that I would like to respond to, but I can say, that since I landed in Liverpool, my reception has been most gratifying to me.

"I regard that reception as an evidence of the kindest of feeling toward my country, and I can assure you, if we go on as good friends and good neighbors, that the English-speaking people are going to be the greatest people in the world. Our language is spreading with greater rapidity than the language of any other nation ever did, and we are becoming the commercial people of the world."

Greece and Rome.

The General's visits to Greece and Rome were very pleasant. "We had," says a friend in the party, "a very interesting time in Greece—most interesting. We saw a great deal of the King of Greece, a bright, interesting young gentleman—who came on board the Vandalia and spent an afternoon with General Grant. They talked a great deal about the relations of Greece and Turkey, and the King was anxious, I observed, to have General Grant's advice as to the best attitude for Greece to take. The King looks a good deal like his sister, the Princess of Wales. He talked English very well, and seemed to be an earnest, resolute man, wrapped up in the success of his little kingdom. He has a hard time, though, between the jealousies of the great powers and the fierce enmity of Turkey.

"When they came to Rome, Cardinal McCloskey called on General Grant and introduced him to the Vatican."

In Russia.

General Grant arrived at St. Petersburg July 30, where he was met by Minister Stoughton. The Emperor's Aid-de-camp, Prince Gortschakoff, and other high officials of the imperial court, called immediately, welcoming the ex-President in the name of the Czar.

On the following day General Grant had an audience with the Emperor. The fountains were played in his honor.

He afterward visited the great Russian man-of-war, Peter the Great. The band played American airs, and a royal salute of twenty-one guns was fired. The imperial yacht then steamed slowly among the Russian fleet lying off Cronstadt, the ships running out American colors, and the sailors cheering.

Subsequently the General had an interview with the Czar at St. Petersburg. The Emperor manifested great cordiality. His Majesty talked of his health and the General's travels, and seemed greatly interested in our national wards, the Indians. At the close of the interview, the Emperor accompanied General Grant to the door, saying: "Since the foundation of your government, the relations between Russia and America have been of the friendliest character, and as long as I live nothing shall be spared to continue that friendship."

The General answered that, although the two governments were directly opposite in character, the great majority of the American people were in sympathy with Russia, and would, he hoped, so continue.

At the station, General Grant met the Grand Duke Alexis, who was very cordial, recalling with pleasure his visits to America.

On the 9th instant he was in Moscow, the ancient capital of Russia, and four days later at Warsaw. At all these places the General was most cordially received.

NAPOLEON WITNESSING THE BURNING OF MOSCOW.

In the Orient.

J. Russell Young, who has been with General Grant in his travels, sums up their visit to China and Japan in the following interesting account: While we were at Hong Kong we visited Canton, which was really our first knowledge of China. The reception of General Grant at Hong Kong was one of the most extraordinary of the trip. There had been a good deal of anxiety about his coming, and the Viceroy sent word that if General Grant preferred it he would have the city closed upon the day of his visit. It is customary in Chinese cities when the Emperor passes through to close all the shops, and the Viceroy thought he ought to pay the General the same courtesy, but General Grant said he wanted to see the people, consequently when he visited the Yamen, the Viceroy's palace, to dine with the Viceroy, it was through a crowd estimated at about 200,000 persons. It was one of the most extraordinary sights I ever saw in my life. The journey was between three and four miles. We went in chairs. I could not have imagined such a mass of human beings, silent, curious, interested, and on the *qui vive*, for " the American Emperor," as they called him, expecting to see a mysterious, supernatural personage, in uniform; disappointed at seeing only a plain, middle-sized gentleman, wearing summer clothes and a straw hat.

From Shanghai we went to Tientsin, where we met the greatest man in China, the Viceroy of that Province, Li-Hung-Chang, who, in addition to the office of Viceroy, also enjoys that of Grand Secretary of State, Guardian of the Emperor, Commander of the Army, and Secretary of War. He had command of the army that put down the rebellion against the Taepings, is of the same age as General Grant, and had expressed the greatest anxiety to see

ELEPHANT WORSHIP IN THE EAST.

the General. The Viceroy is a haughty, imperial person, whose relations with foreigners have never been agreeable; but, in receiving General Grant, he did violence to all traditions of Chinese courtesy and diplomacy, called on him first, gave him dinners, met him at dinners where ladies were present—a thing never known of before in China—and spent most of his time with the General, talking about the Loo Choo question with Japan. The General was very

THE CHINESE WALL.

much impressed with Li-Hung-Chang, who is the most advanced of the Chinese statesmen.

At Peking we met all the leading statesmen of the Chinese Government. We did not see the Emperor, who is a boy seven years old; but we saw, several times, the Prince Regent, Prince Kung. Prince Kung is a Tartar; Li Hung-Chang is a Chinaman.

When General Grant reached Yokohama he was received by members of the Cabinet, Princes of the household, and

WILD ELEPHANTS.

taken to Tokio, about an hour's ride by rail from Yokohama. The Emperor gave him a palace near the sea, where he lived during his stay in Japan, with the exception of the time for two excursions. The visit to Japan was very pleasant in every way. I think that the most important problem in modern politics is the future of China and Japan. I think our foreign policy should be directed more directly to China and Japan than to European countries. I know that it has interested General Grant very much; in fact, I think that if he were questioned on the subject he would say that his experiences in China and Japan were the most important of his whole journey.

General Grant's Return.

General Grant touched his native shores at San Francisco September 20, 1879. To say that he was enthusiastically welcomed by that golden city by the sea is not telling all the truth. The whole country joined in the grand reception extended. The General himself was overwhelmed, and when the opportunity was given his words of thankfulness were lost amid shouts of 50,000 people. It will never be known just what he said on that occasion.

After his reception in San Francisco, the General made a visit to Oregon, where he was also most heartily received. He had been in California and Oregon as a soldier, a quarter of a century before, and was highly gratified, as often stated in his speeches, to find them so greatly improved.

General Grant had now been, practically, around the world. It was exceedingly gratifying to find him enjoying the best of health, and to hear him say, in the widest sense of the phrase:

"There is no place like home."

GENERAL GRANT AFTER HIS RETURN.

In the Yosemite Valley—The "Loveliest Panorama Ever Seen"—Grant's Little Stories.

One of the principal attractions in General Grant's California visit was the Yosemite Valley, which he was permitted to see in all its glory. The scenery and incidents are graphically described by one of the General's companions, as follows:

This has been the first day (Oct. 4, 1879) in Yosemite. The General came to breakfast with Mr. and Mrs. Miller, leaving Mrs. Grant to follow, which she did a little later. The sunlight was stealing down the brown face of Yosemite Rock, the Merced was murmuring over its pebbles, and the trees sighing softly just outside the open windows of the dining room, but he heeded them not. He was too intent on half a dozen mountain trout, which made the principal portion of his breakfast, and which, with green corn, has been the main element of his regimen since he arrived in California.

Breakfast finished, the General discussed his traditional cigar on the front porch. Pending the arrival of the horses which were to take the party up the trail to Glacier Point, Ulysses, Jr., who is becoming almost as much addicted to the cigar as his father, shortened a fragrant Havana. During the delay the ladies had all recovered the roses which they had lost in the long stage rides coming to the valley, and were picturesquely distributed along the front of the hotel.

It shortly appeared that the General would not be accompanied by all his suite. Mrs. Grant during the night had heard some one in the room beneath her saying that the firing of the giant-powder cartridges detached the rocks from the sides of the valley, and wondering that they would risk so dangerous a trip. So she concluded to remain behind with Mrs. Miller, Miss Flood and Mr. Dent. The rest of the company and half a dozen guides made ready for the ascent, and started a few minutes after nine o'clock. The weather was pleasant, but warm.

The General led the line, with Mr. Clark close behind him, as best understanding the region and being the proper person, officially, to be in close attendance. The trail was in shadow during the ascent, but the bright sunlight falling on the opposite side of the valley revealed every point, jutting crag, fissure, and crevice, from the meadows to the summit, and outspread the green valley like a map beneath the feet of the climbing equestrians. The sharp turns of the trail, which is broad and as safe as a wagon-road, brought to view now the upper end of the valley and now the lower.

The General declared it to be the loveliest panorama ever spread out before his eyes. He asked his companion about each point, dome, and canyon as it passed before him in military review. He lamented the dearth of water which should supply the great Yosemite Fall, Nature having been, all about, so lavish of her gifts. He proved so good a horseman that his followers could scarcely keep pace with him. As he came out on prominent points and halted with one or two of those nearest him he looked like a general in war times, inspecting the advance of the enemy, his staff grouped around him.

At Agassiz Column, 2,200 feet above the valley, the party dismounted. At this point many of the peaks had diminished in height; the Cathedral Towers were lost in the more massive forms of the Three Graces; the distance from wall to wall of the valley had grown vaster, and the Merced looked like a narrow ribbon winding through the meadows. The walkers took seats near the edge of the cliffs, which went sheer down 1,500 feet. The General, more venturesome than the rest, stepped out and took a look at the valley from a rock which projected over the precipice. Young Ulysses dared even more. He mounted the rock, and, standing on tip-toe, like Mercury new lighted, reached up, and with a jack-knife cut a large-sized " D " on the trunk of a whispering pine, which, very unadvisedly, had selected that dizzy edge as a place of residence. After once dropping the knife, and having it recovered far down the face of the cliff by the combined exertions of Guardian Clark and his father, he resumed his lettering, which resulted in two neatly chiseled names, that, subjected to a powerful glass, looked very much like " Dora " and " Flora." There was a third which, however was illegible. The young ladies said that they did not care for that kind of immortality, but their protest was unavailing.

General Grant, having finished his survey of the valley, pictorial and strategic, unbent and became talkative. A dog that had followed him up the trail reminded him of other dogs that he had seen and heard of in war-times.

An order, he said, had once been issued during the Rebellion to kill all the bloodhounds in the South, because they were used to pursue rebel prisoners. A soldier, in carrying out the order, found a poodle, and was about to make him a victim of the edict, when a lady, his owner, remonstrated. Said the soldier:

" We are ordered to kill all bloodhounds."

" But he is not a bloodhound," pleaded the lady.

" That may be," returned the representative of military discipline, " but in such times as these no one can tell what he may grow to."

To this he added another brief tale of bravery. Once, the narrator said, he was going from Chicago to St. Louis, over the Alton Railroad. The cholera was raging in St. Louis, and hundreds were dying daily. The car in which he traveled was full, and, the epidemic coming under dis-

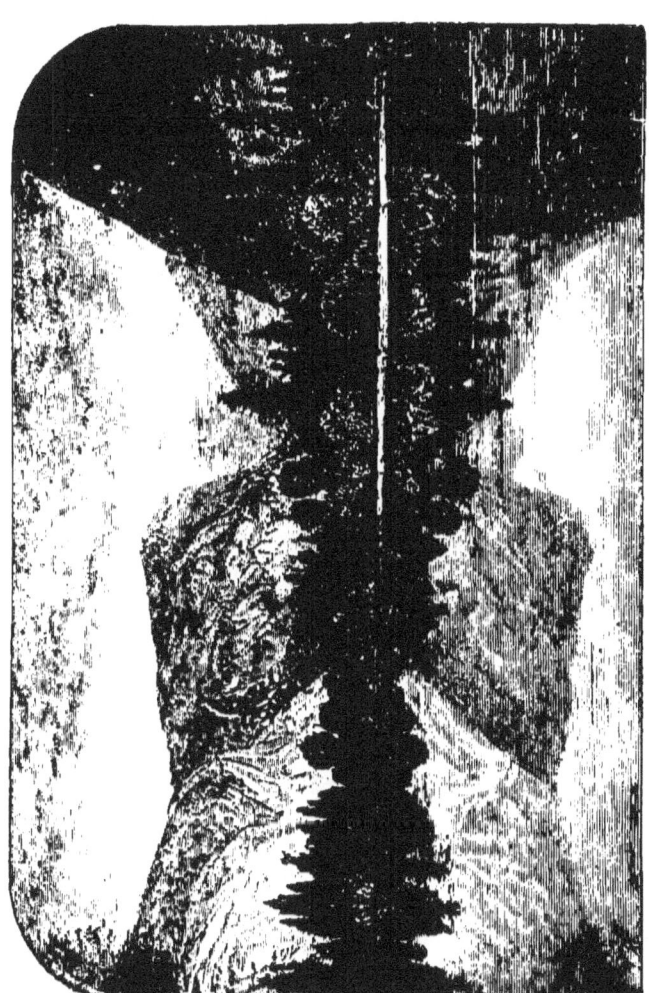

MIRROR LAKE, YOSEMITE.

cussion among the passengers, all expressed themselves as fearless of the disease, and made remarks like these:

"There is very little danger of taking it; in' fact, no danger at all. Those who take it usually get it through fear."

The General admired the courage of the others, and regretted that he was not similarly brave. His self-respect, however, returned, when, having passed Alton, he found himself and another passenger the sole occupants of the car, which was crowded two or three hours before.

After the stories, a cartridge was fired, awaking the echoes for the entire circuit of the valley. Then girths were tightened, ladies and gentlemen remounted, and left the pine to its whisperings and the names to the wasting of the elements. The General led the way to the top of the little house, near Glacier Point, where lunch was to be prepared. Without waiting for it the party pressed on to Sentinel Dome, 1,000 feet higher, or over 4,000 feet above the valley. The General was the first at the top.

The view presents the widest horizon of any point about the valley. There can be seen, close at hand, El Capitan, the Three Graces, the Three Brothers, the Half Dome, North Dome, and Yosemite Rock, with a hundred lesser peaks in the distance. On one side clouds rest, and all the points of Mount Diell group on the other side. Following the course of the Merced, range upon range of mountains, which dwindled into hills and blended with the blue haze that filled the San Joaquin valley, the General scanned every object of interest with a field-glass, which he at last handed back with the remark, that he could see just about as well with the naked eye.

He sat on the rocks, but did not converse with great freedom, the scenery interesting him deeply. Seeing some patches of snow on Mount Diell, he made inquiries about

THE DOMES, ETC., YOSEMITE.

the glaciers. He strained his eyes to behold Mount Diablo and the Coast Range, which possibly might have been visible on a clearer day. Just at this moment there came some puffs of sea breeze, making the air chilly.

Again all remounted, and, picking their way slowly down from the rocky height, a few minutes later were at Macauley's Wayside Inn, where, under the direction of George Lenn, the landlord, lunch was nearly ready. Meanwhile the gentlemen and ladies grouped themselves around the General, on the benches of the back porch, which commanded a splendid prospect of Starr King Mountain, Mount Diell and its brethren, and in the middle ground, far below the spectator, the Nevada and Vernal Falls, thin but lovely sheets of water. Not much could have been expected in a culinary way at this great height, but the lunch was one of the best spread for the Grant party since leaving San Francisco. In its way it was lovelier than the scenery.

The viands discussed, the General disappeared, and, inquiry being made, it was discovered that he had gone to the Point, impatient to see the most superb view of the Yosemite region. Thence can be seen not so much as from Sentinel Dome, but many of the finest rocks and points in the most picturesque attitudes, the upper and most fertile portion of the valley, as far below as the orchards, looking like squares on a checker-board, the apple trees like huckleberry bushes. Beyond, to the horizon, expands the broad, white waste of the high Sierras. Here there were more explosives to awaken specimen echoes. The reverberations made the round of the near peaks of the valley, were tossed grandly from one to another, then passed to the distant mountains, growing fainter, and dying away at last in the region of everlasting snows.

The usual experiment of throwing bottles over the precipice was tried to guage the height by the time occupied in falling. The General tried his hand at throwing, also young Ulysses, who showed great strength of arm. After further diversions at this point, the General was in good humor, and rallied the young ladies, asking them if they were not glad he had brought them.

The descent was made in two hours, the General leading, gaining half a mile in the whole distance. There was a fine succession of views descending, varied from those of the morning by the different position of the sun. The west wall of the valley was in shadow, which grew deeper as the afternoon advanced: the atmosphere was agreeable; a blue haze filled the space within the hills, softening the outline of the rocks, and giving their huge forms beauty and grandeur. Arriving at the level of the valley a few minutes after 4 o'clock. there was a general scattering to hotels. The ascent had been so easy that there had been little fatigue, and there was little complaint of dust. Shortly after reaching the Bernard House the General resumed his cigar as if nothing had happened.

Down in the Mines at Virginia City.

General Grant's travels are of the most varied character. At one time we find him all alone, as was the case in Jerusalem, in the dawn, walking down the narrow street through which the Son of God is said to have carried the Cross; and soon after, in China, he is in the midst of a multitude estimated at 200,000 souls. A few days before reaching Virginia City he is on the summits of the great mountains, and here we find him thousands of feet down under the ground. His descent and amusing experience is described by a friend as follows:

When the General appeared outside in the miner's suit, with his pants tucked in his stocking tops, and with the oldest slouched hat in the building on his head, the party greeted him with "bravos" and a hearty laugh, and Grant, looking with amused astonishment at himself, declared he was ready for Flannigan's ball.

When the ladies appeared in men's suits the laughter was turned upon them. Mrs. Fair had been down before, and Governor Kinkead declared significantly that we all knew the reason why, for in her jaunty sailor's suit she made a pretty picture. The General saw the point, and stepping up, cigar in hand, he said: "I want to offer this young gentleman a cigar." Who has said that Grant is reserved and silent?

On the summit of the Sierras, and sailing over the blue depths of Tahoe, he was always appreciative, and asking all sorts of questions, and to-day, in his miner's suit, and when sure he had escaped curious crowds, 2,100 feet under the ground, he was chatty as a boy, and with a dry humor which did not need Grant behind it to make it good.

He had been very sure that Mrs. Grant would not go down the mine, until finally Mackey offered to bet $1,000 that she would go. In the same joking way the bet was taken by the General, but he did not have the money. It would be useless to apply to a newspaper man for money, he said, and no one else would loan it to him; so, offering some old Japanese coins for security, we started down. But Mrs. Grant did go; and, descending swiftly in the iron cage, we commisserated the General on his loss.

"Well," he said, "a thousand dollars is a good deal of money to lose, but I guess it will stop Mrs. Grant's shopping awhile, and it is the first bet I ever heard of where both sides were winners."

Down we glide as smoothly as in one of your hotel elevators, to the first level, 1,800 feet below. Here we leave our overcoats, which we had put on for the cold ride down the shaft. As the General starts off he calls back to his son:

"Bud, bring some cigars."

"You can not smoke here," says Mrs. Grant.

"Well, I'll try," answers the General, in so emphatic a tone that some one raises a laugh by adding, "if it takes all summer."

Through subterranean and devious paths we follow Mr. Hugh Lamb, the obliging foreman. We examine the vast bodies of ore which we encounter, and General Grant splashes through the water, knocks pieces of ore off with a pick, and is full of curious questions about the cost of mining and milling, the character of the rock, the yield per month, etc., etc. We are getting so far down now that the natural heat of the earth is becoming unpleasant, and Mrs. Grant, who does not seem to enjoy it, says:

"Oh, why can't we have something else for money, and save all this work and trouble."

"Because then it would have to be paper money," answered the General.

Mrs. Grant wants to go back to the surface, but the General says she must not put them to that trouble, and, as all good wives should, she yields, and we leave the ladies in the cleanest place we can find, and go on down. We are soon where the thermometer marks 95 degrees Fahrenheit, and the sweat pours off us. We examine the immense system of timbering, and learn that it has required over $2,000,000 to put this gigantic mine of gold in shape for work. We examine the pumps, and the steam drills with their noisy clatter are stopped and run so that the General may see how they work. Mr. Mackey, who has been through this many times, says it is not warm, but the rest of us sweat and gasp. The General is delighted with the "good sweat" he is having, and getting the attention of the crowd, he says to Mr. Fair: "There are two newspaper men here and plenty near at hand. Find the hottest place you can and let us leave them there." The newspaper men say never a word. Again we take the cage, where it seems cold as a winter's day, and down two hundred feet deeper into the earth we go. Here it is 120 Fahrenheit. Workmen, bare to the waist, come forward, saying:

"General, we have got you here and you will have to shake."

"I like to shake a healthy man's hand," the General says, as he looks at their splendid muscular development.

The water coming from the earth here is so warm that you can not bear your hand in it, and men can only work a few minutes when they are cooled off with ice.

The General thinks it would be a good plan to sentence convicts to work eight hours a day down here. "Anyhow," he says, red in the face from heat, and wiping his face, "this is the place to leave the newspaper men."

"Would you not leave the politicians, too?" asked Governor Kinkead.

"Yes, but there ain't room for all that ought to be put here," the General replies, without a smile, and maybe he meant it. But we can not stay here, it is too warm, and so we make our way safely to the upper and cooler regions.

A Speech of Gen. Grant over 2000 Miles Long—From San Francisco to Galena—What He Said.

In passing from San Francisco to Galena General Grant was everywhere most cordially welcomed home. Such an ovation has never been witnessed before in the western country. The General's remarks, at the numerous towns and stations on the way, were most felicitous, and invariably called out the ringing cheers of the multitude. We give a number of the principal speeches by the way:

Farewell to San Francisco.

GENTLEMEN OF SAN FRANCISCO: The unbounded hospitality and cordiality I have received since I first put my foot on the soil of California has taken deep root in my heart. It was more than I could have expected, and while it has entailed some little fatigue at times, I assure you I have only been gratified for it. I have previously been in California and on the Pacific coast, but have been away a quarter of a century, and when I landed here the last time I found that none of the pioneers had grown old, but if I should remain another quarter century 1 might be compelled to confess that none of you had grown old [applause] and I want to see you again in your prime and youth. Gentlemen, in taking my departure I want to thank you all for the farewell reception given me this evening, and to express the hope that whether or not I am to have the happiness ever to visit your city again, I shall at least meet one and all of you elsewhere, and if it should not be in this life that it may be in the better country.

At Sacramento.

Of all the hospitality bestowed, all the honor conferred, there has been nothing so grateful to my heart as the receptions I have received at the hands of the people here. I would not say what has been done abroad. It has been all that could be done to mortal, but it has not been done for me. It has been done for the people whom I see before me,—for the people of a great country that is recognized abroad as one of the greatest countries in the world. If we all—every one of us—could see other countries, as I have seen them, we would all make better citizens, or, at least, the average of our citizens would be better.

At Fremont.

GENTLEMEN:—I am very glad to see you, but your towns in Nebraska are too thick for me to talk at every place the train stops. They are springing up here so rapidly that I scarcely know the country in passing through, although I have been out here three times before. This is my fourth trip.

"A good many years since I saw you, General," sang out an old farmer in the crowd. "I was with you in Mexico."

"That was a long time ago, my friend," responded Grant, "but we are young men yet."

"I am over 70," said the farmer, as if doubting that proposition.

"I am in the fifties yet," responded Grant, pleasantly.

At Omaha.

LADIES AND GENTLEMEN OF NEBRASKA AND OF OMAHA:—It would be impossible for me to make any number of you hear a word if I had anything very special to say. It is cold and windy, and there are multitudes waiting, and I will only say a few words, and that to express the gratification I feel at meeting you all here to-day. I state to you in addition how glad I am to get back once more upon American soil. Wherever I have been in all my travels in the last two and a half years, I have found our country most highly spoken of, and I have been, as a sort of representative of the country, most elegantly entertained. For the many kindnesses that I have received at the hands of foreign nations and foreign Princes, I feel gratified myself, and I know that all of you do. The welcome given to me there has been a welcome to this grand Republic, of which you are all equal representatives with myself. As I have had occasion to say several times before, since my arrival in San Francisco, we stand well abroad, infinitely better than we did twenty years ago, as a nation and as a people; and as a result of that to-day the credit of the United States in the European market is higher than that of any country in the world. We are there more highly appreciated than we appreciate ourselves. [Applause and laughter.] Gentlemen, I say again that am highly gratified at meeting you here to-day, and thank you [Applause and cheers.]

At Burlington.

MEMBERS OF THE SCHOOL BOARD AND SCHOLARS OF THE CITY OF BURLINGTON:—It gives me great pleasure to meet you and see five thousand or more of the school children of the City of Burlington, and I think if there ever is another war in this country it will be one of ignorance versus intelligence, and in that battle the State of Iowa will achieve a great victory. Furthermore, I think that war will be one of ignorance and superstition combined against education and intelligence, and I am satisfied that the children here will enroll in the army of intelligence and wipe out the common enemy, ignorance. I thank you for your kind attention.

At Galesburg.

LADIES AND GENTLEMEN:—It would be impossible to make myself heard by all of you, or a large portion of you, even if I was in the habit of public speaking. I will do no more, therefore, than thank you for turning out at this time of night to welcome me on my way to my home, and I will say to you that in the two and a half years that I have been away from you I have had a very pleasant time. I have seen a great many pleasant people, and I have been very well received at every place I have been as a mark of respect and honor to the great country which you helped to make up, but as I have had frequent occasion to say since my return to my own country, I appreciate the welcome which I receive from the sovereigns of my own country above all other receptions that they gave us elsewhere. I have had the pleasure of seeing the people of Galesburg but on one other occasion. I passed through in 1868, when I thought all the people in the city were about this spot I am very glad to see you all again to-night. (Applause and cheers `

At Home.

MR. MAYOR, AND LADIES AND GENTLEMEN OF GALENA:—It is with extreme embarrassment that I stand here to-day to receive the welcome which you are according me. It is gratifying, but it is difficult for me to respond to what I have just heard and to what I see, properly, I can say that since I have left here, more than eighteen years ago, it has always been a matter of pleasure to me to be able to return again to Galena. [Applause.] Now, after an absence of two and a half years from this city, having been in almost every country north of the equator, it is with special pleasure that I return here again to be greeted by the citizens of this city, Jo Daviess County, and the surrounding country. In my travels abroad, as has been alluded to by the speaker who has just sat down, I have received princely honors, but they have been honors due to my country, and due to you as citizens and sovereigns of our great country. [Cheers.] It but requires a person to travel abroad, and to get an insight of life in all of the foreign countries, to appreciate how happy we ought to be with the country we have here. It makes better Americans of us all to see the struggling there is, particularly in the Far East, to gain what would be a starving support in our own country. It should be a gratification to us to feel that we are citizens of this country, where want is scarcely known, and where the question of subsistence is not one we think of now. Fellow-citizens I renew to you my thanks for your presence and for the welcome which I have received at your hands. [Prolonged applause and cheers.]

After making the circuit of the globe, we now take our leave of the great General, at his home, with the bending skies above as his real and perpetual arch of triumph.

ARCH DE TRIUMPH, PARIS.

THE
AUDIPHONE

A NEW INVENTION

THAT ENABLES

THE DEAF

TO HEAR THROUGH THE MEDIUM OF THE TEETH, AND
THE DEAF AND DUMB TO HEAR AND
LEARN TO SPEAK.

INVENTED BY
RICHARD S. RHODES.
CHICAGO

Sold Only by
RHODES & McCLURE,
Methodist Church Block, Chicago.
1879.

THE AUDIPHONE!

PRICE.

Conversational Audiphone.   -   - $10,00
Opera   "   -   -   -   15.00

SENT BY MAIL OR EXPRESS TO ANY PART OF THE WORLD ON
RECEIPT OF PRICE.

ADDRESS

RHODES & McCLURE, Methodist Church Block,

CHICAGO.

R. S. RHODES.   J. B. McCLURE.

CONTENTS.

	PAGE.
The Audiphone	3
The Deaf and Dumb can Hear and Spark	4
Directions for Use	4
A Word for the Very Deaf	5
Firmly Fitting False Teeth All Right.	5
Lay Aside the Ear Trumpets	5
To Learn to Speak	7
Opera or Concert Audiphone	7
Hon. Joseph Medill's Testimony	7
John H. McNeely's Testimony	8
From the Chicago Tribune	9
" Inter-Ocean	10
" Chicago Times	12
" Faderneslandet	14
" Die Deutsche Warte	15
" Drovers' Journal	15
" Interior	16
" Advance	16
" Standard	17
" N. W. C. Advocate	17
" Alliance	18
" Living Church	18
" Herald and Presbyter	19
" Evening Wisconsin	19
From Prof. Fay, in the Annals of the Deaf and Dumb	20
Additional Testimony	29, 36

	PAGE.
From the Watchman	21
" Lawrence Journal	20
Personal Commendations	21
E. F. Test to Hon. Joseph Medill	21
E. F. Test to Rhodes & McClure	21
From Bishop Clarkson	22
" A Young Lady	22
" John Atkinson	22
" W. W. Evans	23
" Henry Milnes	23
" S. H. Weller, D.D.	23
" E. C. Ely	24
" B. H. Mulford, Esq.	25
" G. H. Paine	25
Interviews with the Deaf and Dumb	25
Chas. P. Day	25
Alexander Meisel	26
L. M. Larson	26
Alva Jeffords	27
Samuel F. Wood	27
Patented Throughout the World	28
How to Procure an Audiphone	28
The Price of the Audiphone	36
New and Popular Books Published by Rhodes & McClure	37, 38
Rhodes & McClure's Star Guide	39

THE AUDIPHONE.
GOOD NEWS FOR THE DEAF.

An Instrument that Enables Deaf Persons to Hear Ordinary Conversation Readily Through the Medium of the Teeth, and those Born Deaf and Dumb to Hear and Learn to Speak. How it is Done, Etc.

The Audiphone is a new instrument made of a peculiar composition, possessing the property of gathering the faintest sounds (somewhat similar to a telephone diaphragm), and conveying them to the auditory nerve, through the medium of the teeth. *The external ear has nothing whatever to do in hearing with this wonderful instrument.*

It is made in the shape of a fan, and can be used as such, if desired. (See fig. 1, page 4.)

When adjusted for hearing, it is in suitable tension and the upper edge is pressed slightly against one or more of the upper teeth. (See figs. 2 and 3, pp. 4 and 5.)

Ordinary conversation can be heard with ease. In most cases deafness is not detected, it being generally supposed, as is the experience of the inventor, that the party deaf, is simply amusing himself with the fan.

The instrument also greatly facilitates conversation by softening the voice of the person using it, enabling—even in cases of mutes—the deaf party to hear his own words distinctly.

Those Born Deaf can Hear, and the Dumb are enabled to Learn to Speak.

Mutes, by using the Audiphone according to the directions on page 6, can hear their own voice and readily learn to speak.

DIRECTIONS FOR USE.

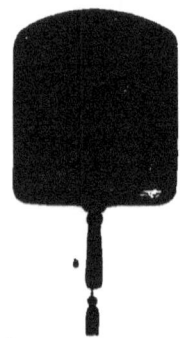

Fig. 1. The Audiphone in its natural position; used as a fan.

Fig. 1 represents the natural position of the Audiphone, in which position it is carried (by gentlemen) by attaching it by means of a hook or button to the vest or inside of the coat, where it will be convenient for use and fully concealed. The shape and flexibility of the disc render the Audiphone an excellent fan.

Fig. 2. The Audiphone in tension; the proper postion for hearing.

Fig. 2 represents the Audiphone in tension and ready for hearing. It is put in this position by means of the silken cords which are attached to the disc, and which pass down as a single cord under the "wedge" in the handle. By opening the wedge (as seen in Fig. 3) the cord, which now moves freely, should be drawn down until the disc is brought to the proper tension (as seen in Fig. 2) when the wedge is closed and the instrument is held in the position required. Experience will regulate the exact tension needed for each person, and also the tension necessary for different voices, music, distant speaking, etc. In this respect the Audiphone is adjusted to suit sound as an opera glass is adjusted to suit distance.

Fig. 3.\ The Audiphone properly adjusted to the upper teeth; ready for use. (Side view.)

Fig. 3 represents the position in which the Audiphone should be held for hearing. It should be held loosely in the hand and its upper edge should be placed in easy contact, by a slight pressure, against one or more of the upper teeth, that are the most convenient. In many instances the "eye teeth" give the best results, but a little practice will soon determine the best for hearing. The *lower teeth should not come in contact with the Audiphone*, nor should the Audiphone be pressed beyond the point of tension at which it has been adjusted, as seen in Fig. 2

NOTE.

A Word Concerning the Very Deaf—False Teeth—And those Using Ear Trumpets.

Persons who have been *very* deaf for many years, and who are accustomed, wholly or in part, to interpret sound by the movement of the lips of the party speaking, may not readily distinguish the *words* of the speaker when *first* using the audiphone, though the *sound* of these words will be distinctly heard. In all such cases a little practice will be required to enable a deaf party to rely wholly upon sound. Such persons should request a friend to read aloud while they (the listener) should carefully observe the words (as spoken) in a duplicate book or paper. When this is properly done the deaf person will be surprised with what distinctness every word is heard by the use of the audiphone. In this way they *educate* themselves to articulate sounds, and soon learn to hear well without observing the movements of the lips.

Persons having false teeth, if they fit firmly, can, notwithstanding, use the Audiphone successfully.

It should be further noted, that persons using such instruments as ear trumpets, etc., which in all cases increase the deafness by concentrating an unnatural force and volume of sound upon the impaired organ, should at once lay aside all such devices on receiving the Audiphone. Such persons, thus accustomed to the *unnatural* sound, through the ear trumpet, will require some practice to again familiarize themselves with the natural sound of the human voice which, the Audiphone always conveys.

TO LEARN TO SPEAK.

Mutes will learn to speak by holding the Audiphone against the teeth, as above directed, and practice speaking while it is in this position.

A good exercise is for the mute, at first, to put one hand on the instructor's throat, watch the motion of his lips, while his other hand is on his own throat, the instructor meantime holding the Audiphone to the mute's teeth. The mute will *feel* the influence of the sound on his hand in the instructor's throat, imitate it in his own throat, will *hear* the speaker's voice on the Audiphone and will be aided in imitating the speaker by *seeing* his lips, and will also hear *his own voice on the Audiphone*, and readily learn to speak.

It is remarkable how rapidly they learn to distinguish words by sound. In a very short time, they have learned to repeat whole sentences spoken to them while blindfolded. It is believed that every mute child may hear and learn to speak by using the Audiphone.

OPERA OR CONCERT AUDIPHONE.

An Instrument of nearly Double Power, for Concerts, Lectures, Sermons, Operas, etc. Also well Adapted for Mutes.

The Opera or Concert Audiphone consists of two discs, each about the shape of the Conversational, as shown in Fig. 1, page 4 (with one disc a little larger than the other) fitted into the same base, a quarter of an inch apart and separated at the upper edges the same distance, sufficiently to be evenly adjusted to different teeth, so that each disc may act independently of the other, and presenting in all respects (except the handle) the appearance of a double Conversational Audiphone. The upper edge of each disc is set against *different teeth*, thus giving the vibration of a whole disc to each tooth and thereby almost doubling the power, and enabling the deaf person to hear music, sermons, lectures, concerts, theatres, operas and public speaking generally, at a greater distance.

The Opera or Concert Audiphone is the best adapted for mutes, not only because the sound received is of greater volume and more distinct, but also the voice of the mute when spoken between the discs is very considerably intensified, and therefore the more distinctly heard by himself.

FROM THE HON. JOSEPH MEDILL.

IN THE CHICAGO TRIBUNE.

(Date, August 26, 1879.)

"It is known that the editor of this paper has been deaf for a number of years, and that during that time he has used all the devices for improving his hearing that he could hear of or that were brought to him. None of them were, however, satisfactory. He has tried the audiphone for some weeks, and finds that it not only improves his hearing

BUT RESTORES THE SENSE

of hearing to him. Not merely does it answer when engaged in conversation with a person who is a foot, or a few feet, from him, but it answers perfectly at a concert. Each note of the musician and each tone of the singer come as clearly and distinctly as they did before the sense of hearing was impaired. Others have also tested this instrument, and have expressed themselves satisfied with its working."

FROM JOHN H. McNEELY TO A. T. HODGE.

(One of the Proprietors of the Evansville [Indiana] Daily Journal.)

OFFICE OF EVANSVILLE JOURNAL CO.,
EVANSVILLE, Ind., Sept. 25, 1879.

Mr. A. T. HODGE,

Firm of Clarke, Friend, Fox & Co., Chicago.

Dear Friend:—I got back this morning all right, and want to tell you about the "Audiphone." Our City Editor, Mr. Allison, tried it, and pronounces it *the* thing. Say to Mr. Rhodes that he hears the very lowest tone of voice, and says it is the only thing of the kind he ever saw that would enable him to hear. He is very proud of it, and sends his thanks.

Mr. G. W. Shanklin, Managing Editor of the *Courier*, was in this afternoon. He is, if anything, more deaf than Mr. Rhodes, and as soon as he tried it he said he heard the conversation of all in the room. I thought he put it in his mouth too far, but when he placed it against his eye teeth he complained that the sound was like a cannon and he could not stand it.

Respectfully, JOHN H. McNEELY.

TESTIMONY FROM THE CHICAGO TRIBUNE.
(Date Sept. 4, 1879.)

The Audiphone—A Most Satisfactory Test.

"In the parlors of the First Methodist Church yesterday afternoon, Mr. R. S. Rhodes, the inventor of the audiphone, submitted his instrument to some severe and very interesting tests, in the presence of a number of people, including Mr. G. C. Tallerday, of the *Medical Times*, Dr. T. W. Brophy, Prof. Swing, Mr. L. M. Stone, and Mr. Gray, of the *Interior*.

Already *The Tribune* has contained a brief account of this wonderful invention, and the interest it has awakened among deaf people is but a revival of that over the announcement made a year or so ago by Edison when he declared himself the discoverer of an appliance by which the man or woman whose ears were utterly useless should be able to hear, not only ordinary conversation, but should be able to appreciate the pleasures of music. When Edison failed to fulfill his promises, people generally, and many medical men, too, scouted the idea of ever being able to reach the point which the inventor of the quadruplex telegraph thought he had reached; but Mr. Rhodes, a deaf man himself, when the telephonic diaphragm appeared, caught a suggestion from it, and the result was his audiphone.

It is in shape like a square Japanese fan, and is made of a composition the major portion of which is vulcanite. At the back of this thing there is a cord, stretching from the upper edge to the handle. By means of this cord the instrument is tuned like a violin, and the tension is regulated according to the distance the sound has to travel. The upper edge of this audiphone is placed against the two upper teeth, and the vibrations received on its surface are conveyed by the medium of the teeth, and the nerves of the teeth to the acoustic nerves, and produce upon them an action similar to the action produced by sound upon the drum of the ear.

In addition to experiments made yesterday with people who were not completely devoid of hearing, two boys were made to hear the human voice for the first time in their lives. One, 17 years of age, was deaf and dumb, while the other was about 15, and, although he could speak, he was perfectly deaf. At first the sounds were strange to them, but after a little they signified that they could hear them distinctly, and understand perfectly that they were sounds. Of course, in order that they may comprehend what the meaning of the words spoken is they will have to be taught.

Medical men and others were charmed with the experiments, they admired the simplicity of the invention, and there certainly now appears to be no earthly reason why the deaf should remain deaf."

TESTIMONY FROM THE INTER-OCEAN.
(Date, Sept. 4, 1879.)

News for the Deaf—Complete Success of the Audiphone—Simple yet Marvelous.

"Yesterday afternoon a number of interested gentlemen assembled in one of the parlors of the First Methodist Episcopal Church, on Clark Street, to gather some information relative to the audiphone. This little machine is the invention of Mr. Richard S. Rhodes, of the firm of Rhodes & McClure, and is intended to be used by those who have wholly or partially lost the sense of hearing.

The audiphone is very simple in construction, and without any mechanism. It is apparently a black polished india rubber or " vulcanite " fan, the leaf part being square with rounded corners, the material very flexible, so that the leaf can, if necessary, be bent double. One side has cords attached from the thin end or top of the flap of the fan to the handle. When these cords are drawn tight they curve down the flap or leaf of the audiphone, which is then fixed for use. It is used by the deaf by applying the thin edge of the fan to the four front teeth of the upper jaw.

There were several deaf mutes present, who were experimented upon. Mr. Charles Day was the first of these. Fixing the audiphone to his teeth he repeated quite audibly the monosyllabic sounds "hoo, hoo," which Mr. Rhodes recited to him. To prove that he had not imitated the sounds from watching the illustrator's lips, Mr. Day was blindfolded and then also showed conclusively, by repeating two more sounds, that this was a bona-fide triumph of the audiphone. Without the apparatus Mr. Day could only be communicated with by the deaf-mute sign language. Mr. Day, who is an intelligent young fellow, is enthusiastic with regard to the audiphone. He has for the first time by its aid heard the sound of his own voice. To *The Inter-Ocean* reporter he stated, via the interpreter, that he was satisfied with the audiphone, and repeated the word " water " so as to be understood, which he had learned by means of these "new spectacles for the ears."

A gentleman who was very hard of hearing tested the audiphone and found it of great benefit. Several other experiments were made, and were in each case more or less successful.

Among those who were in the audience were the Rev. Professor Swing, the Rev. L. M. Stone, and Dr. Gray, of the *Interior;* Dr. J. C. Tallerday, of the *Medical Times;* Dr. Brophy, and representatives of *The Inter-Ocean* and other daily journals."

TESTIMONY FROM THE CHICAGO TIMES.
(Date, Sept. 4, 1879.)

Defeating Deafness—Let those who have not Ears to Hear, Hear with Their Teeth.

"Mr. Richard S. Rhodes, a Chicago business man, has been led by his own deafness, a difficulty of twenty years' standing, to make a series of experiments, covering the last six or seven years, in the direction of assisting the deaf by means of vibrations of the acoustic nerve transmitted through the teeth. He has at last perfected an instrument which promises to greatly alleviate the discomfort not only of the deaf, but of those who have to talk with the deaf. This he has named the Audiphone.

It is a plate of a new composition the material being a part of the invention, and made only for it, measuring perhaps eight inches wide by nine long, and provided with a handle. It looks very much like a fan, and can be used as such. The rubber plate is very flexible, and on the under side is a cord attached to the upper edge of the plate and passing through the handle, in which there is a clamp, by means of which the holder can secure it at any point, and thereby hold the plate bent to any desired degree. When bent the handle is held in the hand and the upper edge of the rubber plate is placed under and touching the eye teeth, the under teeth not being allowed to touch it. Any sound which strikes the place produces a vibration, which is transmitted from the teeth to the auditory nerves, and the impression of sound is produced. For different degrees of deafness different degrees of tension are required, and by means of the cord and clamp one can regulate the tension of the audiphone as readily as he can regulate the focus of an opera-glass.

An exhibition of this instrument was given on yesterday afternoon in room No. 20 Methodist Church block. Among the persons present were Dr. T. W. Brophy, Dr. G. C. Tallerday, of *The Medical Times*, Prof. David Swing, W. C. Gray, Ph. D., of *The Interior*, Mr. Stone of *The Northwestern Christian Advocate*, the Rev. S. Gilbert of *The Advance*, and a number of others, among whom were several deaf-mutes. One or two adults who were quite deaf were present. A number of experiments were tried with the deaf persons, with and without the audiphone, and in some cases with eyes bandaged so that the motion of the speaker's lips should be of no assistance. In all cases the deaf persons found they could hear much better with than without the audiphone, and some, in fact, could not hear at all without it.

One of the deaf-mute boys found himself able to hear quite well with the audiphone, but having been deaf from infancy he had never learned the meaning of sound, and unless he could see the speaker's lips, he could not understand English any more than Chinese. A gentleman about thirty-five years old, who could hear but very little, found himself able with the audiphone to hear remarks made in his ordinary tone of voice by Prof. Swing, who, it is well known, is not a loud speaker, and who was sitting at a distance of ten feet. The professor, whose prayers are rarely heard by the remoter portions of his congregation, was anxious to know how far the audiphone would be useful in churches and halls and whether it conferred the faculty of belief as well as that of hearing. Mr. Rhodes declined to recommend his invention as a remedy for skepticism, or as a convenience for people whose hearing was good, but whose seats were too far from the pulpit.".

FROM THE "FADERNESLANDET."

(Scandinavian Paper, Chicago, September, 1879. Translation.)

[The editor of this journal voluntarily interviewed the parties mentioned herein concerning the Audiphone.]

"This instrument has already attracted a good deal of attention, and all agree that it is going to be of immense value for the deaf. The most prominent papers have contained big treatises over the Audiphone, and we could furnish our readers with hundreds of undeniable testimonies concerning the excellences of the Audiphone, but space compels us to be satisfied in giving the following few:

The Hon. Jos. Medill, proprietor of the Chicago *Tribune*, has been deaf for a number of years, and during that time he has been using all devices known for improving his hearing. None of them were satisfactory, but now, when he has tried the Audiphone for some weeks, he finds that it not only improves his hearing, but restores the sense of hearing to him.

The son of Mr. Jacob Kleinhaus, No. 91 Chicago Avenue, has a long time been suffering from deafness. He states, that at a visit at the company's office he could hear very perfectly through the Audiphone, and intends to purchase one.

Frank E. Gerber, No. 127 Twentieth St., and Samuel F. Woods, No. 94 Washington St., also witness the excellency of the tinstrument.

Charles F. Day, No. 755 Michigan Ave., deaf since 1864, can hear somewhat with Audiphone.

John Holland, deaf eight years, residing at No. 791 Hinman St., can hear with the Audiphone.

Frank Luttrell, residing in Cairo, Ill., states the same.

Fred. Stickel, from Delavan, Wis., deaf and dumb, and attending school in Chicago, can hear with Audiphone. Thinks he can not do without it.

Lars M. Larson, a Swede, residing in Springville, Wis., believes that he can learn to hear with the Audiphone.

Alexander Weisel, twenty years old, eighteen years deaf, can hear with the Audiphone."

FROM THE "DIE DEUTSCHE WARTE.
(German Paper, Chicago, Sept. 14, 1879. Translation.)

"Chicago once more ahead! for Richard Rhodes, of the publishing firm of Rhodes & McClure, of this city, who has been deaf for about twenty years, has succceded in bringing to practical use the long-known theory of hearing by means of the bones of any part of the head, and for which the eye teeth, with their delicate nerve system, form the basis of operation. It is a well-known fact that Beethoven, the great composer, used as a substitute for the ear a metallic rod, which he held between the teeth, with the other end resting on the sounding board of his piano, by which means he was able to hear what his brain had produced, and thus reach perfection in music which has rarely been equaled.

We can say with assurance that those denied the pleasure of hearing, and who have a good set of teeth, will no longer be deaf. We have the best evidence of this in our friend, Jos. Medill, the editor of the Chicago *Tribune*, who assures us, that since he is in possession of the Audiphone he does not feel the loss of hearing to such an extent as before, and that he hears with the Audiphone every word spoken or any other noise near him as good as those whose hearing is perfect, and can again enjoy the theater and other public amusements."

FROM THE DROVERS' JOURNAL.
(Chicago, Sept. 10, 1879.)

"Look to your eye teeth, for they are destined to serve as ears to those who can not hear in the ordinary way. The writer saw an Audiphone tried upon a man whom he knows to be as 'deaf as a post,' and was amused to see the expression of surprise steal over his face at hearing the ordinary human voice. Every deaf man, for the comfort of himself and all with whom he comes in contact, should have one."

FROM THE INTERIOR.
(Organ Presbyterian Church, Dated Sept. 18, 1879.)

"I knew it was coming, and have been waiting for it—something which would do for the hearing what spectacles do for the sight." So writes a friend in regard to the Audiphone. But the tests at Methodist Church Block show that the Audiphone does more than this. No spectacles will give a blind man sight, but the new instrument does give a deaf man hearing.

FROM THE ADVANCE.
(Organ Congregational Church, Dated Sept. 11, 1879.)

"Hear, O ye deaf! The "Audiphone" is the name of an instrument, recently invented by Mr. Richard S. Rhodes, of Chicago, which, it is believed, will work wonders for the relief of the deaf. Its construction is as simple almost as that of a Japanese fan, which in shape it resembles. It is a device by which one whose hearing is either wholly or partially lost, may hear—not through the ear—but through the *teeth;* that is, by means of vibrations communicated from the edge of the fan-shaped instrument to the teeth, and through the teeth, and thence to the auditory nerve. We have seen persons hear sounds in this way who never before knew what sound was. If we are not much mistaken, the world will yet build a monument to our friend Mr. Rhodes for the beneficence of his invention."

FROM THE STANDARD.
[(Organ Baptist Church, Dated Sept. 25, 1879.)

THE AUDIPHONE.

We have just examined an instrument, an invention of Mr. Richard S. Rhodes, of this city, which is admirably adapted to afford relief in partial or entire loss of hearing. It has been pretty thoroughly tested by scientific men and others, and ample testimony is borne that the results are eminently satisfactory. In this invention Mr. Rhodes has proved himself a benefactor.

FROM THE N. W. CHRISTIAN ADVOCATE.
(Organ Methodist Episcopal Church, Dated Sept. 10, 1879.)

" Mr. Richard Rhodes, of this city, has invented a simple contrivance by which sound vibrations may be communicated to the auditory nerve through the upper teeth and jaw, so that persons congenitally deaf are able to perceive sounds very much as if the entire auditory apparatus were restored.

The contrivance consists of a piece of flexible polished rubber in the shape of a Japanese fan, which is bent to the proper vibratory tension, and the edge placed against the upper teeth. A trial of the capabilities of the audiphone was made before several journalists and other gentlemen

Sept. 4, on three persons, one of whom had never heard anything, while the two others were partially deaf. The mute was blindfolded and asked to respond to the sounds made with the use of the Audiphone, which he did in a manner to convince all present that he could hear an ordinary vocal tone. The Audiphone enables those who are partially deaf to hear with nearly or quite the perfection of those who are in complete possession of the sense."

FROM THE ALLIANCE.
(Independent. Chicago, Sept. 20, 1879.)

By means of this instrument, those who have been deaf from birth are enabled to hear, and are learning, by simple auxiliary instructions, to talk.

FROM THE LIVING CHURCH.
(Protestant Episcopal Church Organ.)

"Mr. Rhodes, of the well-known publishing firm of Rhodes & McClure, booksellers, has wandered outside his sphere of selling books into the field of invention. It is called an Audiphone, and really possesses the most wonderful qualities. By a simple contrivance, a square-cornered fan of special composition, people as deaf as the traditional post are enabled to hear quite clearly. For the old fashioned ear, the *teeth* are substituted and the same end arrived at. Experiments made the other day with persons deaf and dumb from their birth, proved beyond question that the invention is a decided success. Both vocal and instrumental sounds were heard by those who had never heard before."

FROM THE HERALD AND PRESBYTER.

(Organ Presbyterian Church, Cincinnati, Sept. 17, 1879.)

"There is no limit to the inventive genius of man. Not until the past few years have the people been almost constantly startled by new and strange things. The latest is a curious device for relieving deafness, based upon an entirely new principle in the transmission of sound to the auditory nerve.

"The inventor, Mr. Richard S. Rhodes, of the publishing firm, Rhodes & McClure, of Chicago, who was very deaf, discovered that he could hear his watch tick while holding it in his teeth, whereas he could not when placed to his ear. This led him to begin a series of experiments, which we are told proved entirely successful, and resulted in the invention of a cunningly-devised contrivance, which, when held in the teeth, gathers the sound and communicates it to the brain.

FROM THE EVENING WISCONSIN.

MILWAUKEE, Oct. 1, 1879.

The editor of this paper, Mr. J. F. Cramer, who is very deaf, after making some experiments with the Audiphone, says, in an editorial, "He has come to the conclusion that the Audiphone is a very valuable invention. His deafness is of long standing and his hearing is very much impaired, yet, with the Audiphone he can hear persons speak at a distance which would be utterly impossible without its use. He has tried it in the process of reading and he finds it equally serviceable. The use of the Audiphone has the advantage that it can be applied without effort and that when a deaf person is disposed to be lazy he can hear notwithstanding. With the old 'snake auricular' this can not be so for there is always a deal of labor in striving to keep the auricular in the ear."

FROM PROF. EDWARD A. FAY.

(Professor in the National Dumb Institute, at Washington, D. C.)

In the American Annals of the Deaf and Dumb.

Experiments with the audiphone have recently been tried upon some of the pupils of the Chicago Day-School and others who are entirely deaf so far as the external ear is concerned, and it is found that they are able to hear and distinguish sounds through this instrument. We are not prepared to say with the enthusiastic reporter of one of the Chicago papers who witnessed these experiments that "there now appears to be no earthly reason why the deaf should remain deaf," for in the many cases of deafness where the auditory nerve is impaired, the audiphone can be of no avail ; but where, as is often the case, the defect is only in those parts of the ear by which vibrations are conveyed to the nerve from without, we believe this invention will prove a great boon.

FROM THE WATCHMAN.

(International Organ Y. M. C. A.)

The Audiphone, a new invention that enables the deaf, even mutes, to hear through the medium of the teeth, was thoroughly tested before the members of the Chicago press last week. The test was in all respects satisfactory.

FROM THE LAWRENCE DAILY JOURNAL.

(Kansas, Dated Sept. 25, 1879.)

The name of Richard S. Rhodes will be held in grateful remembrance as the discoverer of the Audiphone by thousands who may come after him, as will the names of Fulton, Morse, and other inventors and discoverers, who have contributed so much to science during the nineteenth century.

PERSONAL COMMENDATIONS.

(Extracts from Correspondence.)

LETTER TO HON. JOSEPH MEDILL, EDITOR "CHICAGO TRIBUNE."

(From E. F. Test, Claim Agent U. P. R. R.)

{ Freight Auditor's Office,
Omaha, Neb., Sept. 21, 1879.

My Dear Mr. Medill:
Instead of going to church this morning, I have come down to the office to thank you for your renewed thoughtfulness in sending me the pamphlet about the Audiphone. I sent to Mr. Rhodes for one after receiving your first notice, and got the conversational style. It answers the purpose admirably. It has created quite a sensation among my friends. It was comical to see a number of them fanning themselves with it, under the impression that it was simply a fan, and then in a few moments to see their astonishment when they saw me hearing with it just as well as I ever did. All the physicians to whom I have shown it endorse it warmly.

Your sincere friend,

E. F. Test.

FROM E. F. TEST.

(Claim Agent Union Pacific R. R. Co.)

{ Union Pacific R. R. Office,
Omaha, Neb., Sept. 19, 1879.

Messrs. Rhodes & McClure, Chicago, Ill.
The Audiphone came all right yesterday noon. It appears to answer the purpose admirably, and seems to have

created quite a sensation among my friends. Now that I have it, I don't want to do without one for a day. I am astonished and delighted at the volume of sound the instrument can convey through the nerves. It seems to work on the principle of ventriloquism. I enclose my cheque No. 4 on the State Bank of Nebraska for $10.00.

I am, respectfully yours, E. F. TEST.

FROM RT. REV. R. H. CLARKSON, D. D.,
(Bishop of Nebraska, Omaha.)

"I am personally acquainted with Mr. Test of Omaha, and I can scarcely make him hear by shouting to him. If you make that man hear you do wonders."—*Bishop Clarkson's remark while purchasing an Audiphone in the Chicago office.*

FROM A YOUNG LADY.
(Concerning her Father.)

"My father, who has been deaf forty-six years, and who can only hear when you are near to him and speak very loudly, can hear an ordinary conversation by the help of the Audiphone."

CHICAGO, Sept. 22, 1879.

FROM JOHN ATKINSON.
(Sec., Treas., Supt., and Engineer Racine Gaslight Co., and builder of West Side Gas Works, Chicago.)

OFFICE OF RACINE GASLIGHT COMPANY,
RACINE, WIS., Sept. 19, 1879.

Messrs. RHODES & McCLURE, Chicago, Ill.

Gents:—I have been deaf for thirty years, but can now hear distinctly with the Audiphone. I thank God that I now have something that will help my hearing, and that I can now enjoy, as well as others, some of the delights of this world's amusements.

Yours truly, JOHN ATKINSON.

FROM W. W. EVANS.

{ GRANT LOCOMOTIVE WORKS,
PATTERSON, N. J., Sept., 1879.

Messrs. RHODES & McCLURE, Chicago, Ill.,

Gents:—Your Audiphone to hand. The lady (my sister) has tried it, and finds she can hear now an ordinary conversation, which she can not do without it. I would not part with it for ten times its cost.

Very respectfully, W. W. EVANS.

FROM HENRY MILNES, Esq.

(Resident of Cold Water, Mich.)

I have been a little deaf for over thirty years and very deaf for twenty years, and have not heard a sermon, lecture, or a tune on the piano for twenty years. I procured an Audiphone yesterday and can already hear quite well an ordinary conversation, and expect by a little practice to be able to hear sermons, music, etc., without much difficulty.

CHICAGO, Sept. 24, 1879. HENRY MILNES.

S. H. WELLER, D.D.,

"The loss of hearing is a deprivation than which there is scarcely any other more serious. The extent to which this misfortune prevails can only be realized when we reflect that the deaf are to be found in numbers in every community. The man, therefore, who by any device, affords relief to this army of afflicted ones, not only deserves honorable mention as an inventor, but becomes a benefactor of his race. The "Audiphone," recently invented by Mr Rhodes, of the firm of Rhodes & McClure, gives good promise of meeting this case. The inventor himself, with whom it is difficult to converse at all, joins readily, with the use of this instrument, in ordinary conversation. I am satisfied, from experiments which I have witnessed, that, excepting instances in which the auditory nerve is fatally paralyzed, all the deaf may, by its help, be enabled to hear and intelligently converse. This invention employs an entirely new and hitherto unused medium of sound, and hence the most convincing and gratifying results are obtained, where the natural organ of hearing is entirely destroyed. I should like to speak in terms of strong commendation of an invention which is certain to be widely used, and which is bound to play a prominent part in ministering to the comfort of the afflicted."

S. H. WELLER,
Resident Minister, Chicago.

FROM E. C. ELY.

{ OFFICE OF REYNOLDS & ELY,
WHOLESALE PROVISION DEALERS,
PEORIA, ILL., Oct. 4, 1879.

Messrs. RHODES & MCCLURE, Chicago, Ill.

Gentlemen :—The 'phone at hand, and on trial even more satisfactory than could be expected at first use. My wife and friends are delighted and enthusiastic over it. They are rejoiced that I can hear, and I am glad that it no longer requires an effort on their part to enable me to do so. I have sent the pamphlets to friends similarly afflicted, and would like five or six more for the same purpose.

Yours truly, E. C. ELY.

FROM B. H. MULFORD, ESQ.,
(Of Montrose, Pa.)

"I am certain I can understand lectures, concerts, etc., with it. My audiphone is the wonder of the day. It helps me wonderfully in conversation."

FROM G. H. PAINE.

FREMONT, NEB., Sept. 30, 1879.

Gentlemen: Received Audiphone by yesterday's express. To-day I am able to hear ordinary conversation, directed against the Audiphone, from two to four feet distance *perfectly;* Music *clear* in any part of the room. If every deaf person using your Audiphone meets with as complete success as I have they must surely wish you the success the invention merits. To say that I am gratified would only express moderately how I feel.

INTERVIEWS WITH THE DEAF AND DUMB.

CHAS. P. DAY.
(Mute ; residence 755 Michigan av., Chicago, after using an Audiphone a few days.)

Do you hear quite well now with the Audiphone?

"Yes, sir."

Do you hear now, after using the Audiphone for several days, any better than you did when you first began to use it?

"Yes."

Are you learning to speak now by the help of the Audiphone?

"Yes, sir. My mother and friends are teaching me every night."

Do you think you can learn to talk by the help of the Audiphone?

"Yes, sir; I have an Audiphone at home and try to learn.

I can now say about eleven words. I can say "bed," "out," "water," "bad," "bad girl," "papa," "no," etc.
How long have you been a deaf mute?
"Since 1864."
How old are you?
"Seventeen years."
What caused your deafness?
"Brain fever."
Do you believe that mutes, like yourself, can hear and learn to talk with the Audiphone?
"Yes."
Do you believe the Audiphone would be a good thing in the deaf mute institutions?
"Yes, sir; I think so."

FROM JOHN L. GAGE.
(A mute from birth; residence, Winetka, Cook Co., Ills.)

Are you a mute? "Yes sir, from birth. I am forty-six years old. Before I tried the Audiphone yesterday, I never heard sound. I could *feel the jar* of a loud cry, noise, thunder, etc., at a short distance."

Did you ever hear the voice of your mother or sister? "No sir. I have felt the jar of music."

Did you hear Mr. Rhodes when he spoke to you on the Audiphone? "Yes sir, I thought his voice seemed to be a fine sound, which is different from the rough jar felt by the mutes."

Was that the first human voice you ever heard? "Yes sir, it was, and I heard it with the Audiphone."

How did Mr. Rhodes make you hear your own voice? "He pricked my leg with a pin, and I made a mild cry, which I heard through the Audiphone, or from my teeth nerves. I think I can learn to speak with the Audiphone, but I think it is harder for the congenital deaf mutes than the semi-mutes, because they do not know what sound means."

L. M. LARSON.
(Springville, Wis.)

How long deaf? "Eighteen months after birth." Age?

"Twenty-three years."
Can you hear anything without the Audiphone?
"No."
Can you hear with it?
"A little."
Do you think you could learn to hear with it?
"I can, I believe."
Where do you live?
"In Springville, Wis., and am a student at the National Deaf Mute College, Washington D. C."

ALVA JEFFORDS.
(Washington, D. C.)

Can you hear with the Audiphone?
"A little."
Can you hear without it?
"No."
How long have you been deaf?
"Fourteen years."
Do you believe you could learn to speak with the Audiphone?
"Yes."
Do you attend the Deaf and Dumb Institution in Washington? "Yes."

SAMUEL F. WOOD.
(Englewood, Ill.)

"I have been deaf ever since I was about fifteen years old It was caused by swimming and diving too much. I hear some sounds. I hear the sound of the voice, but not loud enough to distinguish words. Occasionally I happen to hear a word or two. Sometimes I distinguish what is said partly by the motions of the lips and partly by catching some sounds."
How old are you? "Thirty-five years."
Can you hear music?
"I hear a sort of sound, but not enough to enjoy it in the least."

Do you hear pretty well with the Audiphone?

"I hear very much better, though not perfectly. I am of the opinion that by practicing with it I would gradually acquire the ability to hear ordinary conversation and sermons. Probably I could never be able to take part in conversation with several different persons either with this (the Audiphone) or with anything."

We think by use constantly you would be. Do you find that it enables you to *control* your *voice*, and that it is easier to speak?

"It is certainly easier to speak, especially for any length of time, with this than without it. I think it worth while to have one just to practice speaking and talking."

Mr. Wood had so nearly lost his voice that it was a great effort for him to speak, and his articulation was very indistinct. After reading a page from a book by the aid of the Audiphone, he remarked that "he read with ease, which he could not have done without the Audiphone."

The Audiphone operates with remarkable power in enabling the deaf to successfully hear the varying sounds and harmonies of music, whether produced by the voice or instruments. To such who have heretofore been denied the pleasure of hearing the "divine art," this invention will be of great advantage. So, also, is it invaluable as an aid to hear sermons, lectures, public speaking, etc.

FROM ABBIE R. STEVENS.

SALEM, MASS., Oct. 9, 1879.

Messrs. RHODES & McCLURE.

Gentlemen:—The Audiphone arrived Monday, and it greatly exceeds my expectations. I hear ordinary conversation with ease, and it is a wonder to me every time I use it. Sounds that I had not heard for years, and had quite forgotten, came back distinctly, and the more I use it the better I like it. I expect to hear in church this winter, which I have not done for five years. You certainly deserve the thanks of all deaf people. ABBIE R. STEVENS.

ADDITIONAL TESTIMONY.

The Audiphone Tested at the Deaf and Dumb Institution at Indianapolis, Ind.

FROM THE INDIANAPOLIS DAILY JOURNAL.

(October 13, 1879.)

Tested at the Indiana Institute for the Deaf and Dumb with Satisfactory Results—A Wonderful Instrument, by Means of Which the Deaf Hear and the Dumb Speak.

"Although this is not the age of miracles, it must be recorded that on Saturday evening last a very wonderful occurrence was witnessed by a party of ladies and gentlemen gathered in one of the parlors of the Institution for the Deaf and Dumb. Literally, 'the dumb spoke and the deaf heard,' and this without the performance of any miracle, the aid of any legerdemain or mysterious incantation. It seemed simple enough, when the feat had been accomplished, and yet twelve months ago it could not have been done—had, indeed, been scarcely dreamed of as a possibility of the dim distant future.

"The scene on the occasion referred to was, it need hardly be said, novel and deeply interesting. Only a few persons were invited to witness it, and included in the select company was a *Journal* representative. The object was to test the value of the newly-invented audiphone to persons who for the greater part of their life have been both deaf and speechless. Mr. Richard S. Rhodes, the inventor, was present to superintend the test, which was the more intensely interesting because it was the first time that the new instrument had been introduced to the pupils of any institution devoted entirely to the education of deaf mutes.

"Before describing the test, it may be well to state for the information of the uninformed reader that the audiphone is an instrument of peculiar composition, made in the shape of a fan, which possesses the property of gathering the faintest sounds (somewhat similar to a telephone diaphragm) and conveying them to the auditory nerve through the medium of the teeth, the external ear having nothing to do in hearing with this wonderful instrument. To aid in the experiment with the pupils, a cabinet organ was brought in use—for the first time, it is understood, in the history of the institution—and a class of girls, varying in age from twelve to eighteen, were provided with audiphones. One by one the children were taken close up to the organ, which was played by one of the lady teachers, and were asked whether, with the use of the instrument, they could distinguish any sound, and if so, whether any difference in sounds was noticeable.

"A bright little girl of ten or twelve years was the first to whom the test was applied. She had not heard her own voice or distinguished any sound for a number of years, and was regarded as stone-deaf and speechless. She had not listened more than a minute when her features lighted up with a smile which told the whole story. It was not that the music was sweet and pleasing—the child's uncultured sense of hearing knew nothing of sweet or harsh sounds—but it was a revelation to her to hear at all. When asked whether the organ music appeared all one tone, her reply in the mute language was, that she could distinguish what seemed to her different sounds; and that fact was all that needed to be established at the first experiment. Several other children listened, and with the aid of the audiphone reported like results, some hearing less distinctly than others, but all being able to distinguish some sound when the organ was played, and noticing the difference when it suddenly ceased. Some of the older scholars and a few of the teachers then experimented with the use of the instrument, until about twenty had tried it. Only one, a male teacher, reported unfavorably, and in his case it was admitted that the auditory nerve was entirely destroyed, rendering it impossible for any mechanical appliance to be available or useful.

"It is a theory of the inventor of the audiphone, and is, indeed, a well authenticated scientific fact, that speech depends upon hearing; in other words, that deaf people are dumb because they can not regulate or distinguish the differences of sound by hearing their own voice. An experiment was therefore tried with a view of inducing a young lady who had not uttered an intelligible sound since she was quite young to speak her own name and some other words. She had been listening, with the aid of the audiphone, for several minutes to others talking, but when asked to say something herself she was very reluctant, and explained in the sign language that she did not like to, because she would only make some hideous sound, which would make her appear ridiculous. Eventually, however, she was induced to make the effort, and although she spoke quite low, being nervous and afraid to talk loud, she heard her own voice quite distinctly. The joy which the young lady felt at this glad discovery can be imagined better than it can be described.

"Another test applied was to repeat two or three letters of the alphabet to the deaf mutes, who were asked if they could distinguish the difference in sound between 'a,' 'i,' and 'ab.' Simple as this may seem to those who have always had full enjoyment of the senses of speech and hearing, it was as difficult to the deaf mutes as it would be for an ordinary mortal to tell at first hearing the different shades of meaning attached to the multiplicity of vowels in the Fiji language. Except in the case of mutes who at some time in their past life have been able to hear and speak, the mind is a perfect blank as to the meaning of sounds, and, therefore, all that could be done at a first trial was to ascertain whether the audiphone enables them to hear with such distinctness as to recognize any difference in sounds, and to this extent the experimental test of last Saturday was quite satisfactory. One of the most experienced teachers in the institution stated to the *Journal* representative, during the evening, that, although he did not think the audiphone would put an end to his occupation as a teacher of deaf mutes, yet he did believe the instrument would prove very serviceable to persons whose auditory nerve had not been destroyed by disease. Those who were partially deaf would doubtless be able to hear with the aid of the audiphone much more easily and correctly than they could with an ear-trumpet; and it seemed evident from what had been witnessed that evening, that many cases hitherto considered hopeless might gain benefit from the new invention.

Mr. Rhodes, the inventor, says he has known of several persons whose powers of speech have been recovered with the ability to hear, and mentions particularly the case of two sisters who had lived together, but had not heard each other's voice for a number of years, who were able during the first hour of using the new instrument to talk quite freely. Until last Saturday Mr. Rhodes had not exhibited the audiphone outside of Chicago, where he resides, and he chose the Indiana institution for his first test, because he recognized the fact that the benevolent institutions of this state are noted all over the country for their progressive management and the excellent educational advantages provided."

FROM THE INDIANAPOLIS DAILY NEWS.

(Oct. 13, 1879.)

Spectacles for the Ears—Interview with the Inventor of the Audiphone—A Boon to the Deaf.

"Saturday afternoon a *News* reporter met Richard S. Rhodes, of Chicago, the inventor of the audiphone, a device that enables the deaf to hear through the medium of the teeth, and the deaf and dumb to hear and learn to speak. The external ear has nothing whatever to do in the hearing with this instrument, and in this respect it differs from all other helps to hear. In shape the audiphone is simply a large square Japanese fan, made of carbonized rubber, on the back of which is a cord stretched from the upper edge to the handle. By means of this cord the instrument is tuned, and the tension is regulated according to the distance the sound has to travel. Mr. Rhodes, when accosted by the interviewer, had one of these fans. He has himself been deaf for twenty years, unable to hear only the loudest noise. He placed the upper edge of this rubber fan against his two middle upper teeth.

"'This fan,' he said, 'responds to vibrations just as the drum of the ear does. Sound is communicated to the brain and understood, as it produces the same vibrations on the auditory nerve as are produced through the medium of the ear. Of course the deaf mute has to be taught what these vibrations are. When they can understand them they can hear by this instrument, and can talk, as the audiphone enables them to hear their own voice and to modulate it.'

"'How long have you been thinking about this instrument?'

"'Four or five years. The first were put on sale July 26, of this year. I had only a hundred made at first, and have had thus far only 1,300 manufactured. When I got the first lot of the audiphones I took a ten-year old boy, a deaf mute, not extra bright, either, home with me, and in two weeks, with little more than half an hour's instruction each evening, I taught him to understand the alphabet, to count as far as ten, and quite a number of small words. Any one who knows the difficulty of teaching deaf and dumb children will appreciate this rapid progress. There are now deaf and dumb children in Chicago who, by means of this instrument, can hear and repeat whole sentences. The movement of the lips have nothing to do with it, for they can hear as well blindfolded as with their eyes open. The Princess of Wales is deaf. I sent her an audiphone a while ago. She probably got it last week. The son of John Bright, the great English statesman, while in Chicago, a short time ago, bought two. A gentleman bought one of me to send to a missionary in Turkey. Several have been sent to San Francisco. A lady and a gentleman of this city each have one. The gentleman is E. T. Johnson, an attorney here. I will show the audiphone at the Indiana Institute for the deaf and dumb this evening, the first institute of the kind at which it will have been exhibited. I am convinced that the first institution that introduces it will be the first to teach by articulate sound. Deaf mutes can comprehend music before everything else, by means of this instrument, and can measurably enjoy it.'

"'Mr. Rhodes, your audiphone seems to be as wonderful as that instrument told of by Thomas Hood in his Tale of a Trumpet, " I sold her a trumpet, and the very next day she heard from her husband at Botany Bay."'

"'Ha! ha! The instrument is not wonderful. I don't claim that; it is simple. I haven't been trying to sell any great number of them yet. People will find out what it is. You have no idea of the amount of correspondence I already receive. There is seemingly no end to the inquiries. I have had it patented everywhere and can afford to let it advertise itself. I certainly can make a fortune out of it in seventeen years. There are some persons, perhaps one in ten, of those called deaf mutes, to whose infirmity this invention can afford no help. It is those in whom the auditory nerve has been destroyed by disease. False teeth do not stand in the way of using the instrument if the plate fits tightly. Can I hear through the telephone? Oh yes, with this fan in my teeth. I hear the patter of the rain outside now, and the street noises. I can not hear whispers. The sounds must be articulate. The more I draw up this string at the back the more and the sharper the vibrations. I need to draw it up considerably to hear a bass voice distinctly. It is somewhat easier to understand female voices.'

"A bent piece of metal, a tuning fork to teeth and several similar experiments first gave Mr. Rhodes the idea of his instrument. Saturday evening he showed it at the parlors of the deaf and dumb asylum, several of the pupils manifesting unbounded delight upon discovering that they could hear music and the tones of the human voice. One young lady who had not spoken since she was quite a child was induced to attempt to pronounce her name. She did so with the audiphone to her teeth and was overjoyed to find that she could hear her own voice."

FROM THE INDIANAPOLIS DAILY SENTINEL.
(October 14, 1879.)
The Audiphone—How it Works.

"Mr. Cox, the agent for the new instrument called an audiphone, explained its workings to a *Sentinel* reporter yesterday. It is astonishing that it has only been invented so recently.

It consists of a sheet of carbonized rubber, about 8½ by 10 inches in size, to which is attached a handle. From the top of the fan extends a couple of cords, which are brought down and held by a small fastener in the handle. By this the tenston can be increased or diminished at pleasure. The edge of the fan is placed between the teeth, or allowed to rest on them, and the sound of a voice from in front passes over the fan to the teeth, and from thence to the auditory nerve, thence through the bones of the face.

A deaf and dumb person can hear by means of this simple instrument, and of course can learn to speak. It will do away with the necessity for the aslyums over the country for such unfortunates. For the worst cases there is an additional sheet of a smaller size placed on the under side of the instrument, to assist in conveying back to them the sound of their own voices.

The experiments made at the asylum on Saturday were highly satisfactory to all parties. The cost of the audiphone is $10 for the simple, and $15 for the compound."

Letters patent for the Audiphone have been secured throughout all the world.

The instrument can be procured by enclosing the price, and addressing

RHODES & McCLURE,
Methodist Church Block, Chicago, Ill.

PRICE:

Conversational Audiphone, - - $10.00
Opera Audiphone, Extra Power, - 15.00

www.ingramcontent.com/pod-product-compliance
Lightning Source LLC
Chambersburg PA
CBHW031747230426
43669CB00007B/515